90 Days *of Devotions* AND *Prayers*

90 Days of Devotions AND Prayers

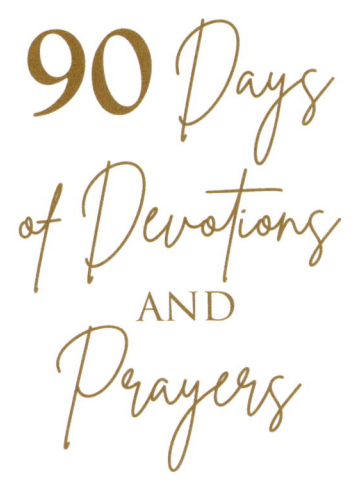

by

LIONESS RISING LADIES' MINISTRY

TRULY LOVED MEDIA
JER 31:3

Jacksonville, Florida

90 Days of Devotions and Prayers

Copyright © 2024 by Lioness Rising Ladies' Ministry

All rights reserved by the author under the International Copyright Law. No part of this book may be reproduced in any form without the permission of the author.

Unless otherwise noted, scripture quotations are taken from the King James Version®. This translation of the *Holy Bible* is in the Public Domain, except for in Great Britain.

Scripture quotations marked as NASB are taken from the New American Standard Bible®, Copyright © 1960, 1971, 1977, 1995, 2020 by The Lockman Foundation. Used by permission. All rights reserved. lockman.org

Scripture quotations marked as BSB are taken from the Berean Standard Bible, which is in the public domain.

Scripture quotations marked as NKJV are taken from the New King James Version®. Copyright © 1982 by Thomas Nelson. Used by permission. All rights reserved.

Scripture quotations marked as ESV are taken from the ESV® Bible (The Holy Bible, English Standard Version®). ESV® Text Edition: 2016. Copyright © 2001 by Crossway, a publishing ministry of Good News Publishers. The ESV® text has been reproduced in cooperation with and by permission of Good News Publishers. Unauthorized reproduction of this publication is prohibited. All rights reserved.

Scripture quotations marked as NIV are taken from THE HOLY BIBLE, NEW INTERNATIONAL VERSION®, NIV® Copyright © 1973, 1978, 1984, 2011 by Biblica, Inc.® Used by permission. All rights reserved worldwide.

ISBN-13: 979-8-9853467-5-6
Printed in the United States of America.

Published by:

Truly Loved Media
www.trulyloved.media

Dedication

This book is dedicated

to all who thirst.

(Isa 55:1)

Preface

These devotions were collected from the voice of many waters (women), and they are a love project of the Ladies' Ministry of Living Waters World Outreach Center in Fernandina Beach, Florida. The Holy Spirit asked our women to write a book of devotions, and we have obeyed. We are honored that you have chosen to spend the next three months traveling through the pages of this book and it is our prayer that the Holy Spirit will minister to you in powerful ways.

Please take the time to look up and meditate on the scripture(s) that are provided for each day. Well into the project, the Holy Spirit gave one of our women a vision of the book cover. It clearly said, *90 Days of Devotions and Prayers*. We had not planned to include a prayer for each devotion, but prayers quickly became a part of the plan. Slow down and ponder each prayer with the Holy Spirit. You may find that what is provided is simply a jumping off point for more prayers to flow from your heart to His.

In Genesis 17:17 (NASB), Abraham begged the question: "And will Sarah, who is ninety years old, give birth to a child?" Heaven's answer was a resounding yes! Whether you are new to believing God for a promise to be fulfilled or, like Sarah, you have become advanced in years in the waiting process, we bless you and pray that at the end of these 90 days you find yourself refreshed, expectant, and full of faith that God will bring to the moment of birth AND deliver (Isa 66:9).

Come, all you who are thirsty,
come to the waters;
and you who have no money,
come, buy and eat!
Come, buy wine and milk
without money and without cost.

Isaiah 55:1 NIV

Day 1
Finish

Have you read the Preface? If not, please take a couple of minutes to do so!

I had breakfast with a new friend today. During our time together, the subject of this devotional project came up. By this time, I had begun to collect entries from women, but had lost steam. She simply said, "Finish it." That's a tiny, yet powerful, sentence. It's one that bears repeating, so I think I will, for your benefit and for mine — finish it! After she threw that sucker punch my way, I heard words coming out of my mouth that I knew weren't my own. I said something like, "Jesus is the Author and the Finisher. He's a finisher; not a quitter. He finishes what He starts." How about you? Do you have any God inspired projects lying around barely done, half done, or almost completed? If so, finish it. It's easy to begin "God ventures" with great zeal and enthusiasm, but somewhere along the way, when they lose the luster of newness or roadblocks appear, excitement can tend to wane. At this point, we're well on our way to finishing these ninety devotions, but there's still more work to do before this book is placed into your hands. Today's prayer is for our team as much as it's for you. If the Holy Spirit has given you a project that you have left by the wayside, pray with me, and may we see the projects we've been entrusted with to completion!

Initially, because of the subject matter at hand, the first entry, "Finish," was going to be the last devotion of the book. But, today, I felt the nudge to move it to the beginning; the last shall be first!

**Proverbs 16:3   Colossians 3:23-24
Hebrews 10:36   Ecclesiastes 7:8**

90 Days of Devotions and Prayers

Prayer: Holy Spirit, please give us endurance and help us finish all the projects that You inspired us to begin. Help us to be finishers, just like You. Show us the path of grace and mercy for each of our assignments so that we not only finish, but finish well.

Day 2
The Makings

Every life has within it "the makings" of great stories to be shared with generations to come. These makings consist of those areas of life that try to keep us awake at night: a medical or financial crisis, a prodigal child, a badly fractured marriage, and the list goes on. Woven into our hearts is the very real desire for a knight in shining armor to come to our rescue. However, when it comes to problems faced by loved ones, or ourselves, most of us want to quickly and single-handedly fix the problem at hand. The desire for a rescue is great, but it is mixed with the desire to take matters into our own hands. Most of the best rescues I've known of — whether in situations I've observed, a movie, a book, or the Bible — involved a major crisis and a last-moment rescue. I think it's the "last moment" part of the equation that bothers us most. The real challenge is the waiting period that is involved, along with the fear of what might happen if we don't insert ourselves into the rescue plan. The Holy Spirit once spoke to my heart, "Waiting is a form of worship." Don't look at your flesh's inactivity, as doing nothing. See it as He does, worship! It's a sweet smelling aroma to His nostrils, and it accomplishes more than your flesh ever could!

2 Chronicles 20

Prayer: Holy Spirit, please help me to look at every troubling situation in my life as "the making" of a great story to be retold to generations to come. Help me to allow Jesus, my personal knight in shining armor, to come to my full and complete rescue. Fill me with hope for my situations at hand, and help me to know, in advance, that waiting for You is well worth the wait.

Day 3
Stirring the Pot

When you step out in obedience to the Holy Spirit, know that you are stirring the enemy's pot. You may see evidence of this in the form of what looks like the same ol' yucky stuff happening in your life, but in an increased or heightened manner. Or maybe a few less than desirable situations have been added to your already full plate. If this is the boat you find yourself in, take heart and be of good cheer! The resistance is only evidence that the enemy is shaken, and he is stepping up his game in an attempt to shake you! Instead of reacting to the reactions of the enemy — smile, it's a weapon! Even if there appears to be nothing to smile about, by faith, you are smiling at the future! Your smile is a display of faith (Prov 31:25)! So, even if the boat you are currently in seems to be sinking under the weight of it all, raise a hallelujah up the mast and remember Who is sleeping in the boat with you! Lie back on the chest of that One, relax, and enjoy the ride to the other side! When it's all said and done, He will give you something to smile about!

John 16:33   **Isaiah 54:10**
Luke 8:22-25   **Philippians 1:28**

Prayer: Holy Spirit, even if it seems forced, by faith, please help me to smile in the face of what seems like insurmountable circumstances. Help me to lean against You in a position of surrender, trust, and confidence in Your great love for me.

Day 4
Great Ball of Fire

This morning my husband and I woke at a predawn hour to secure an outside table on the second floor of one of our seaside restaurants. It was dark when we arrived, so we used the light from our cell phones to read the menu. We had a leisurely breakfast over great food and conversation, all the while, staring at the view in front of us, anticipating what was sure to come.

Along the way, an interesting party of four was seated next to us, and I was drawn into their conversation. It was all about Jesus and things that interest me greatly. I began to multitask. I was busy gazing at the view in front of me, all the while eavesdropping on the conversation beside me. I soon deduced that the young man next door was a pastor, and he was beginning to share a recent sermon with his breakfast buddies. I was hooked and shifted my attention and gaze to the table next door to hear what the young man had to say. After all, he could share a key that might help in my current set of circumstances.

After a few minutes of this, I suddenly became aware of the lunacy of what I was doing and felt the Holy Spirit impress something on my heart that I knew wasn't just for that morning. It was an encouragement to not get so consumed with what others are preaching online or writing in books about Jesus that I don't take enough time to hear what He wants to say to me personally. This is what I heard:

*"Keep your gaze and your attention on Me,
not on what everyone else is saying about Me.
There are many voices in the land, but don't lose sight of MINE."*

PSALM 119:105   PSALM 63:1

90 Days of Devotions and Prayers

Prayer: Holy Spirit, with all that is available through my phone and other resources, help me to keep my focus on Your Word and on what You are speaking to me, personally. Cause me to yearn to wake up each morning to spend time with You in worship, in Your Word, listening to what You want to speak to my heart, and sharing my heart with You.

Day 5
Spirit Surfing

One Sunday after Church, my husband and I took our son to the beach. It was a beautiful summer day, the tide was high, and the conditions were perfect for boogie boarding. My son and I waded out with our boards. We gave it a go, but soon found it tougher than we thought to catch waves at just the right moment to ride them effortlessly to shore. I noticed to get the best ride, you must get past the breaking point of the waves. In the middle of our boogie boarding attempts, I couldn't help but think of how what I was experiencing in the water was also true of how we walk out our lives with the Holy Spirit. To catch the biggest waves, or opportunities of the Holy Spirit, you must be willing to push past what you think is your breaking point. Pushing through waves to get to placid waters can be hard work. You're fighting against the waves, the current, and passing other surfers to reach the stillness of the sea.

After some time, my husband walked past me and said, "I'm going to help him catch a wave." Isn't that exactly what our Helper, the Holy Spirit, wants to do for us? WHAT GOOD NEWS, WHAT GRACE! We aren't expected to get ourselves into the perfect position for catching His waves of opportunity. We cooperate with the Holy Spirit, but He is the One Who guides us into deeper waters, past the turbulence of life, to receive from Him. Once we are there, we must embrace the mystery of the deep and the timing of our stay there. Avoid the trap of looking around to see other surfers being launched more often and quicker than you. There is much to be learned in the deep; lessons that are not available in shallow waters. The Holy Spirit customizes the wave we are to ride and the exact timing of launching us onto it. Our job is to allow ourselves to be towed into the deep, to rest on our board, ready and waiting for His push, and then to ride the glorious wave to whatever shore He has planned for us.

Psalm 42:7

Prayer: Holy Spirit, help me to quit fighting to get past the breakers in my life. Help me to trust that You are more than capable of getting me to where I need to be. Help me to trust that Your timing to "launch" the plans that You have for me is much more perfect than my own. The plans are Yours, not mine, so help me to release them back into Your hands and at the same time, be willing to play my part in seeing them come to pass.

Day 6
Esther's Poem

You Chose Her

You chose her
   an orphaned beloved
   adopted in Your perfect love

You chose her
   favored by the King
   and destined to be Queen

You chose her
   innocent as a dove
   well taught to know Your love

You chose her
   to call Your people to fast and pray
   believing You would make a way

You chose her
   a trusting child to seek Your face
   so she would know Your time and place

You chose her
   to boldly speak the truth
   then murderous Haman no longer ruled

You chose her
   to rescue Your nation
   from Your enemy's annihilation

You chose her
 to bring divine turnaround
 showing the world Your renown

You chose her
 for her time in history

And for such a time as this
 You chose me

The Book of Esther

Prayer: Heavenly Father, just as You chose Esther to be born for a particular time and place, thank You for choosing me to be born for such a time as this. Holy Spirit, help me to become a bride who has made herself ready to fulfill her divine destiny and calling. Help me to receive the favor You have bestowed upon me and help me to be obedient in saying what You ask me to say and doing what You ask me to do.

Day 7
A Life Built for Two

There's a bicycle built for two parked outside a beachside rental shop in my hometown. Every time I see it, I'm reminded of a similar bicycle that my family owned when I was a child. I remember pedaling around with my girlfriend on that bicycle. Whoever was in front had the responsibility of steering, a fact that was a little scary for the person occupying the back seat! Both cyclists had the responsibility of pedaling; however, the back seat pedalist often took it a little easy in the pedaling department. Our life should be like that bicycle built for two. Allow Jesus to occupy the front seat position and take full advantage of your seat behind Him. Loosen the grip on your "handles," ease up on the pedaling, and enjoy the ride!

Matthew 11:28–30   Amos 3:3

Prayer: Holy Spirit, please help me to relax and enjoy my life's journey with You. Help me to grow so confident in Your ability and desire to get me where I need to go, that I'm happy to allow You to steer and do the heavy pedaling. Help me to trust that as my faithful Father, You want me to get where I'm meant to go, right on time, all in one piece, more than I do!

Day 8
Reflections

One day I was resting on my sofa, and an old high school annual caught my attention. The name of my high school was printed in a material that looked like a mirror. As soon as I saw it, this word came up from my spirit: "As in a mirror, face reflects face, so the heart of man reflects man." As we spend time in His presence, we are transformed by the renewing of our minds. The more time we take to be transformed, the more we will reflect the beauty of His nature.

2 Corinthians 3:18   Romans 12:2

Prayer: Holy Spirit, please help me to spend focused and unrushed time in Your presence so that I am transformed and become a beautiful reflection of Your glory.

Day 9
Self-Talk

Be mindful of how you talk to yourself. If you're unkind and unloving to yourself, how do you expect to be kind and loving toward others?

Proverbs 12:18   **Ephesians 4:29**
Mark 12:31   **Proverbs 23:7**

Prayer: Holy Spirit, please help me to be mindful of the self-talk that I engage in each day. If I begin to speak disparaging words about myself to myself, please prick my heart, and help me to stop. Then, help me to speak Your truth, what You say about me, to myself!

Day 10
Liquid Love

When God's love is poured out, it runs from the top of our heads to the soles of our feet and fills EVERY crack and crevice. Liquid Love. It has a strong, intoxicating fragrance that evokes a passionate response. What do we do with it? We love others and leave behind His fragrance.

Song of Solomon 1:2-3

Prayer: Holy Spirit, help me to receive Your liquid love, live in the reality of it, and splash it on all who come in contact with me.

Day 11
Consult Me

It is very important to consult with Me. My direction will always lead to life. I may not always give the answer you would like to hear, but My ways are not your ways and My thoughts are higher than your thoughts. I see from the beginning to the end. Do not consult mediums, but come to Me, for I delight in speaking with you and guiding you.

Proverbs 3:5–6   **Isaiah 55:8–9**
Leviticus 19:31   **Psalm 32:8**

Prayer: Holy Spirit, please help me to relinquish control of my life's decisions to You. Help me to trust that You care about my life and the decisions that I must make. Help me to grow in learning how You guide me and then, help me to follow Your leading, even if it wasn't the way I was planning to go.

Day 12
Row

Rowing a boat can be hard work. During long races, oars become heavy, muscles begin to burn, and the temptation to quit may become very real. Don't abandon your oar. Look for waves of mercy as you row. Mercy may present itself in the form of help from others. Invite other "oarsmen," into your boat and form a team. Being a Christian was never meant to be an autonomous endeavor. We are meant to be a part of the church and, in most cases, we can accomplish much more as the Body of Christ than as individual body parts. In the sport of rowing, a person called the coxswain sits in the stern of the boat facing the rowing team. His job is to steer the boat and make sure the crew is rowing in rhythm and to their full potential. He is like a coach and a cheerleader rolled into one. In addition to inviting other oarsmen into your boat, invite the Holy Spirit in as the coxswain. He can steer, instruct, train, and cheer better than any individual oarsmen or all of them combined. Don't abandon your oar! Ask others to join your crew, and ask the Holy Spirit to take the helm as coxswain. Keep rowing; the waters are about to part for you.

Proverbs 27:17   1 Corinthians 1:10
Hebrews 10:25   Psalm 133:1–3

Prayer: Holy Spirit, please help me to look for, recognize, and receive the waves of mercy that You have surrounded me with. Show me the crew that You would have me to row with and help us to row together in unity and in power. Holy Spirit, please be our coxswain. Help us to focus on and heed Your training and instruction. Cheer us on individually, and as a team, in ways that encourage and inspire us to not only finish our race, but to win it (2 Cor 2:14, 1 Cor 15:57, 1 Cor 9:24)!

Day 13
Pursue, Recover All

In 1 Samuel 30, David finds himself suffering at the hands of Israel's ancient enemy. Amalekite marauders have kidnapped the wives and children of David's mighty men and in their distress, they are threatening to stone David, their leader. David's initial reaction is not one of faith. The Bible says that he "was greatly distressed" (1 Sam 30:6). Fortunately, David had discovered a valuable secret from all his years of adversity in the wilderness. He "encouraged himself in the LORD his God" (1 Sam 30:6).

And it's here, in this place of desperation, that he hears the promise of God. "Pursue: for thou shalt surely overtake them, and without fail recover all" (1 Sam 30:8).

Have we unearthed this secret in our wilderness experience, this hidden gem? We must encourage ourselves in the Lord and allow our roots to sink down deeply into His rich soil. When we draw near to Him in the hard, dry places, then we too, like David, will hear His voice of promise: "Pursue…without fail, recover all" (1 Sam 30:8).

Isaiah 41:10   Psalm 31:24   2 Timothy 1:7
Romans 8:31   Isaiah 43:2

Prayer: Lord, help me to hear Your promises for my life. Thank you that You give me strength to pursue, to recover, and to receive all that You have purposed in Your heart for me. Today I believe Your Word and my heart cries with the sweet psalmist of Israel, "Blessed be the Lord, Who daily loadeth us with benefits, even the God of our salvation" (Ps 68:19).

Day 14
Presence

My presence isn't just a feeling. It's a knowing, a truth, a promise.

Hebrews 13:5b   **John 15:4**

Prayer: Holy Spirit, regardless of whether I feel it or not, help me to walk in the confidence that Your presence abides within me and that I carry Your presence with me everywhere I go.

Day 15
Father of Lights

Father of Lights

You are the rightful God upon Your throne
You are Creator of everything our eyes have known

You are Almighty – King of Kings
The One who takes care of Your own

You are the Lord of Love
Who shines upon our path each day
With thankful hearts, we praise Your holy name

James 1:17   1 John 1:5–7

Prayer: Father, thank You that You are my Father of Lights Who gives good and perfect gifts to me, Your dear child. Please help me to lift my vision higher to not only see You seated upon Your throne of grace, but to see myself seated with You, seated in the lap of luxury of Your goodness and Your grace. Help me to walk in the light of Your love today that I might have sweet fellowship with You and my fellow man.

Day 16

Divine U-Turn

Last night, I left our local high school's cafetorium for what was most likely the last time. My husband and I were there for a drama production put on by our daughter's theater class. As I was leaving, I was tempted to go down the long and winding road of despair. You see — high school, for my daughter, has not been a fun experience, to say the least. It has been a hard road and easily the hardest four years of my life, not to mention hers. I was comparing her high school years to mine and all the other "normal" teenage girls I could think of. I'm familiar with the dangerous terrain of this landscape, and yet there I was, headed down a path that I knew wasn't good for me and I was offering very little resistance. But then, as I walked out of the building, I saw a little, single yellow flower blooming out of dirt. Instantly, I was reminded of the beloved book, *Hinds' Feet on High Places*, and the lesson that Much Afraid learned during her journey down into the desert. It's the lesson of "Acceptance with Joy". Just as quickly as I was headed down the road to destruction, the Lord offered me a "U-turn," of sorts. I picked the little flower to represent my choice to, once again, take the hands of Sorrow and Suffering on this journey of mine into the Kingdom of Love. As I picked the flower and walked to our car, the Lord reminded me that all the sorrow and all the suffering is not for naught, but for His glory. Instead of despairing, I suddenly felt comforted and encouraged to continue on the path that He has chosen for me — a tailor-made path equipped with everything needed to transform my life from that of a trembling "Much Afraid" into a life defined by His Grace and Glory.

Recommended reading: *Hinds' Feet on High Places* by Hannah Hurnard

JOHN 11:4   MATTHEW 7:13–14   ISAIAH 61:1–3

Prayer: Holy Spirit, when I am tempted to despair, please help me to make a divinely inspired U-turn that helps me to put my trust in You.

Day 17
Don't Hurry, Be Happy

Slow down so that you have time to "fill up," with the oil of the Holy Spirit. This infilling enables you to pour out the gifts you have been entrusted with. This filling and pouring process will bring great joy! Just as physical exercise requires commitment and time, so does spending time with Jesus and exercising our spiritual gifts. We must empty ourselves and our busy schedules before Him to activate, or reactivate, the grace gifts that the Holy Spirit has given us. They flow out of an intimate relationship with Jesus, and this requires time. Don't spend your time carelessly, and don't allow your giftings to go to waste. They were made to bring great fulfillment to your life and to bring help and encouragement to others. As we spend time with Jesus and exercise what we have been entrusted with, we paint a glorious picture of His heart and the love that He has for others. Encouraging others will encourage us and lead to happier and more fulfilled lives. In a world that screams, "Hurry up," we must be intentional about slowing down.

1 Corinthians 12

Prayer: Holy Spirit, thank You for being the perfect gift giver and thank You that You have chosen the gifts that suit me best. Help me to slow down and spend time with You each day, and help me to recognize the gifts that You have placed within me. Show me how they are best demonstrated through my life, and help me to lavishly pour them out in a way that blesses others and Your heart. Cause me to be so satisfied in my relationship with You and who You created me to be so that I genuinely celebrate the giftings of others, as well as my own.

Day 18
Mountain Discernment

Not every mountain you see are you to climb. I have given you hinds' feet for specific mountains. Those mountains will crumble under your feet, become as dust, and be carried off by the wind.

Habakkuk 3:17–19   Exodus 14:14
Isaiah 29:5

Prayer: Holy Spirit, please give me discernment to know which mountains You have given me the authority to climb unto victory. Help me to not despise the climb, but to learn from every upward movement. Please coach me on my way up, help me remain teachable to the very end, and once I have reached the pinnacle, help me to help others who have been given similar mountains to climb.

Day 19
A Life Well Spent

Yesterday, I had the privilege of attending the funeral of a woman named Lydia, whom I had never met. She was a mentor and spiritual mother to my pastor and spiritual mom. I rode with my pastor to the funeral and was so blessed by the worship, the words that were spoken, the people I met, and the meal that was served. Before attending the funeral, the Holy Spirit impressed on my heart that Lydia's life was a life well spent, and her funeral certainly echoed that sentiment. The concept of "spending my life," has been rolling around in my heart and mind. I'm seeing my days as currency. I'm buying something with how I choose to spend them. I've thought about how we often encourage people to "look at the bigger picture," and in many situations, I see the wisdom of that. However, the past couple of days I've been inclined to "look at the smaller picture." I'm taking notice of the fact that the years of my life consist of months, which consist of weeks, which consist of days, which consist of moments. I feel the Lord's encouragement to remember that a life well spent consists of thousands upon thousands of moments well spent. So, these days I'm focusing on the moment at hand and asking the Holy Spirit to help me live in "the moment," and to "buy gold," even with what may seem like life's most insignificant or mundane moments. I'm asking Him to help me not be so focused on the next season that I miss all the opportunities afforded me in the one I'm presently living in. At the end of the funeral service, someone said that there was a legacy in the building — Lydia's legacy. My pastor is a part of that legacy, and I am a part of hers. Lydia's life was a life well spent; she invested wisely in her relationship with Jesus and others. May the same be said of each of us. Every moment matters.

Ephesians 5:15–16

Prayer: Holy Spirit, please help me to remember to live each moment of this day to its fullest potential regardless of what I'm doing. Give me a daily revelation of the impact that my choices have on the future. Remind me to live in the day I have been given, not in those gone by or those yet to come.

Day 20
Glory of Eden – Break Out

While worshipping to the song "Glory of Eden," by David and Nicole Binion, a revelation came to me. The Glory of Eden is being restored within us so that it can be released out of us. Sit or stand with the song and ponder Eden. Ask the Holy Spirit to help you visualize the garden, and allow its breathtaking beauty to fill your senses and imagination. Ask that a longing for the beauty of Eden be released into, and through, your life.

Proverbs 4:23

Prayer: Holy Spirit, please fully occupy my heart with the Glory of Eden, so much so that it overflows into the people and places around me. You are the Master Gardener. Help me to tend the garden of my heart so that it issues forth the glorious beauties of Eden.

Day 21
Lift Your Vision Higher

In relinquishing the care of your loved ones to the Father, I share with you a phrase that I learned from my spiritual mother, "The lesser is included in the greater." In other words, when I pray for what is on His heart, He will take care of "the lesser things," that are on my heart. This doesn't mean that I never pray for loved ones or personal needs, but it does mean that my whole prayer life is not consumed with "self." Allow the comfort of this to FREE YOU UP to truly partner with God in intercession, trusting that HE will perfect the (lesser) things that concern you.

Psalm 138:8   Hebrews 7:27
Romans 8:24

Prayer: Heavenly Father, please help me to loosen my grip on the concerns that I have for my family. Help me to pass the care for each one into Your capable hands, trusting that You can perfect each life in a way that my human understanding and effort never could. As a mother and a wife, if there are prayers that I need to pray, please lead me in intercession so that my prayers effectively partner with the intercessions that You are making for us.

Day 22
Fulfillment

You lack nothing, for I am your fulfillment. I never run dry.

**Psalm 23   Ephesians 2:3–10
Isaiah 49:15**

Prayer: Holy Spirit, please help me to return to the well of living water all throughout my day for encouragement and fulfillment, instruction, and correction (John 4:10–14).

Day 23
The Key of Peace

These are words from your Heavenly Father: "When I speak, I speak peace. It's not rushed. It will bring clarity. When waters are raging, you will find Me walking on top of them. I am peace! Invite Me to come and be your peace. Let's dwell here, live from here, and witness from here. When bad news comes, receive from the place of peace. My peace will take you places where peace is the key. You cannot enter these places without the key of Peace."

Psalm 85:8   John 14:27

Prayer: Holy Spirit, please help me to shod my feet with the Gospel of peace, so that everywhere my soles step today, I walk in peace and carry peace into the lives and situations that I am faced with.

Day 24

Mighty Man of Valor

In the Book of Judges, chapter 6, we find Gideon in the shadows, threshing his family's wheat behind the winepress. Israel's enemies, the Midianites and the Amalekites, had been terrorizing them for seven long years, causing extreme conditions of poverty and dire distress. It's in this national crisis that the Angel of the Lord addresses God's chosen (yet cowering) hero in a new light: "The LORD is with thee, thou mighty man of valour" (Judg 6:12). At this point, Gideon is anything but brave. In fact, it takes a supernatural fleece to convince him otherwise — but God does prevail. Gideon realizes that it is the Lord of Hosts, Himself, Who is calling him out of the darkness.

How many times have I been like Gideon, full of doubt and fear, only to hear the Holy Spirit whisper to my heart, "Fear not; for thou shalt not be ashamed: neither be thou confounded" (Isa 54:4).

Yes, it is the Lord of Hosts, Himself, Who is calling to us, as well. May we, like Gideon, heed His call.

Joshua 1:9

Prayer: Lord, open my eyes to see Who it is that is with me — the Holy One of Israel, the LORD of Hosts. Each day, Your faithfulness is my success; for surely, "Thy gentleness hath made me great" (Ps 18:35). You make my feet like hinds' feet and set me on the proper path for my life. I am Your loving and grateful daughter of mighty valor.

Day 25
In the Secret Place

In this life, we encounter tribulations and face many battles; however, there are also times when we don't need to fight. The true battle lies in seeking refuge in God's presence, in the secret place, allowing the storm to pass. Isaiah 26:20 says, "Come, my people, enter thou into thy chambers, and shut thy doors about thee: hide thyself as it were for a little moment, until the indignation be overpast." There are times when enduring tribulation simply means standing firm on the Word of God in the midst of our wilderness experience. Regardless of our circumstances, we must find our sanctuary in God and hide ourselves in Him.

Often, instead of fighting with our shield and sword, all we need to do is resist the devil, and he will flee. This act of resistance is our response, much as it was with David, who ignored the enemy's voice (Ps 38:13). Sometimes, it requires even greater strength to stand firm on God's Word and character, waiting for His salvation, than to engage in battle. Though heat and drought may come, God will sustain us through it all.

Kathryn Kuhlman said, "Sickness can come to anyone, so can disaster and misfortune. But in most instances, they are only temporary." Storms will arise and dissipate. Temptations and tribulations will come, but they will not destroy us if we continually dwell in the shadow of the Almighty. Consider Jesus and His disciples in the boat during a fierce storm. The tempest was terrifying, yet no harm befell them. Today, seek refuge in the embrace of Almighty God and find your peace in Him.

Isaiah 58:11   2 Chronicles 20:17
Psalm 91   Isaiah 45:3   Jeremiah 17:8

Prayer: Holy Spirit, when I face trials, teach me to hide in You and seek Your face. When I'm at my lowest, show me treasures hidden in darkness and encourage me to stay hidden in You, especially if I'm tempted to lose faith or to escape my trials by anything other than Your grace.

Day 26

Lily

This morning I awoke with Lily on my mind. Not my beloved granddaughter, Lilly, but Lily, the Saint Bernard. I found this Lily on a YouTube video I watched to kill a little time and to escape reality for a few minutes. Lily's story is not unlike that of many people. It was quite tragic until someone came along and rescued her. This rescue was no small feat. A great deal of time, energy, and thousands of dollars had to be invested in her care. It wasn't the tragic story that was resting on my mind this early morning, but, rather, the words of the man who rescued Lily. His short confession spoke to my own soul as he said, "Lily isn't the smartest dog in my pack, but she has something better. She has my heart. She's the one I look forward to coming home to, and she's the one I regret leaving behind, knowing that she'll spend her time sitting quietly at the door, awaiting my return." I hope the Lord feels the same towards me. I woke up thinking how blessed Lily is to have a master who loves her so unconditionally. I was struck by the truth that she didn't have to do anything to earn her owner's love. He loves her just as she is, a big, clumsy Saint Bernard that loves him in return.

1 JOHN 4:19   PSALM 18:16–19

Prayer: Holy Spirit, please help me to be Your faithful friend who carries Your beautiful heart. Help me to receive the fullness of Your unconditional love, just as I am, without having to do anything to earn or maintain it.

DAY 27
Give Them to Me, Watch and See

This prophetic word came to me during worship at church, Sunday morning. I shared it with the congregation, and now I share it with you:

We can have such a tight grip on our children and it hinders their walk. I felt the Lord say, "Tell them to release them to Me." We can impose such a controlling spirit over them, thinking they should look or act in a particular way. The Lord says, "I have them right where I want them. Watch what I will do; I will amaze you. Have you not remembered My promise? You do not see as I see. I see their heart, their beginning to the end. Now, release them to Me!"

EXODUS 6:1   EXODUS 14:13–14
1 SAMUEL 16:7

Prayer: Holy Spirit, please help me to fully surrender my children's welfare into Your beautiful grace and care. Help me to remember the promise that You perfect the things that concern me, and that all Your promises are Yes and Amen (Ps 138:8 and 2 Cor 1:20). If I begin to attempt to exert control over my children in an unhealthy way, please show me and help me to quickly relinquish them back into Your care.

Day 28
Go With the Flow

A few years ago, I was having a conversation with a good friend. She was traveling with her two daughters and two dogs to West Virginia, a ten-hour jaunt from her island home. She was headed to a fiftieth birthday celebration for her sister. Her mother, other siblings, and extended family would be present for this milestone event. As she traveled, I began to contemplate events like the one she was headed into. Occasions for great joy are often mingled with annoyances and opportunities for great offense. While I pondered, the following thought came to mind. It's a good reminder for any of us headed into a similar situation. If the celebration doesn't go as planned, oh well, go with the flow. If things go in a direction that cause your heart to become angry, say to your heart, "Heart, BE GLAD!"

I think we can all relate to much anticipated events that don't go exactly according to plan. Usually, these annoyances come in the form of our personal preferences being violated because the event isn't going according to OUR plan. When that happens, adjust your sails, go with the flow, choose the road of humility and preferring others, and watch for the Holy Spirit to do interesting things that would not have happened otherwise. Rather than forming "alliances" with likeminded/disgruntled attendees, seek to be a peacemaker in situations that seem anything but peaceful!

Colossians 3:12   Ephesians 4:2   James 4:6   James 4:10   Matthew 5:9

Prayer: Thank you, Holy Spirit, for much anticipated events that I am blessed to be a part of. Help me to loosen my grip on the idea of event perfection, and replace it with thoughts of loving others well and enjoying the event, even if there are hiccups or unexpected surprises. Help me to be a peacemaker who inspires peace in the hearts of others.

Day 29

Mum's the Word for this Mum!

Recently I was in the middle of enabling an adult child in an area that is not unfamiliar. Along with the enabling, I was considering a conversation I would have with him to "straighten out" the problem at hand, AGAIN. At times like this, I tend to forget that none of my other well-planned conversations did the trick. In the middle of this situation, the following came through as a text from a friend who had no idea what I was struggling with. It said: "When your grown children don't want to listen to you, stop talking. Life will teach them; let them go." And remember, in the story of the Prodigal Son, the Father let the wayward son go.

Luke 15:11–31

Prayer: Jesus, You are the Way, the Truth, and the Life. Help me to release my children to Your love and trust that although human words don't reach them, one encounter with the Way, the Truth, and the Life will forever change them.

Day 30
Don't Give the Enemy Rest

Concerning our thought life:

> If our thoughts are in rebellion against God,
> If our thoughts are in unbelief or fear,
> THEN the enemy is at rest in our minds.
> Don't give him rest!

Romans 8:7–9   2 Corinthians 10:5
Philippians 4:8   James 3:17

Prayer: Holy Spirit, please help me to be mindful of my thoughts. When thoughts come that are contrary to Your Word, please help me to cast them down and replace them with truth. Help me to renew my mind to line up with the realm of the Spirit, instead of the mind of the flesh.

Day 31
Overwhelmed

If I made the following statement, how would you interpret it?

"I am overwhelmed."

If I could somehow take a poll, I bet that over 90% of responders would say it means they have too much on their plate, they're surrounded by negative circumstances, or maybe, a colossal combination of both. I've been pondering how often we give the word "overwhelmed" a bad rap, and I'd like us to have a shift in our thinking about the word. From this day forward, may we think of the word "overwhelmed" in a positive light. If we take time to be overwhelmed by the goodness of His presence, we will find ourselves less overwhelmed by life's circumstances and more overwhelmed by His presence with us.

Philippians 4:8   Psalm 61:2

Prayer: Holy Spirit, regardless of how much is on my plate, please help me to prioritize time in Your presence. That way my circumstances don't have the ability to overwhelm me, because I'm completely overwhelmed by Your presence.

Day 32
Host

You are hosting someone's presence. Whose presence will you choose to host today?

Joshua 24:14–15   Ephesians 4:27

Prayer: Holy Spirit, please be my special guest today. Help me to be the most wonderful, inviting, and accommodating host that You have ever known.

Day 33
Silence

Silence is not always a place of not hearing. We tend to feel left out or lonely when our world has grown silent around us. We say, "God, where are You?" He says, "Silence is a place where I speak and you listen." Listen for the sound of silence.

1 John 5:14–15   Psalm 116:1–2
Psalm 18:6

Prayer: Holy Spirit, please help me to grow secure in my relationship with You so that if it feels like You aren't as talkative as in past times, I am able to rest against Your chest and enjoy Your company knowing that You ARE the Word. When the space we are in is void of many words, help me to avoid nervous chatter and just rest, wait, and listen for Your voice.

Day 34
Forsaken Not

Regardless of your current circumstance, you are not a forsaken woman. You are not, you are not, you are not! There is One who will never leave you or forsake you. Run into His arms for comfort, for love, for mercy, and for the experience of His faithfulness. Enjoy the embrace of this Bridegroom King, the One who is ever faithful to His bride. He longs to gather you into the full embrace of His arms. It is your safe place, your haven from the storm. You are not rejected or abandoned. You are loved, you are admired, and you are worthy.

**Genesis 28:15   Hebrews 4:16   Hebrews 13:6
Joshua 1:5   Joshua 1:9**

Prayer: Heavenly Father, please remind me that You are the God Who sees me. Help me to live in the truth of that fact, whether I feel it or not. In this place of feeling abandoned by others, help me to resist the temptation to withdraw from the One who will never leave or forsake me. Help me to run to the comfort of Your warm embrace instead of chasing after lesser gods who promise a quick but temporary fix for my feelings of loss and abandonment.

Day 35

Dustin

The death of a child can leave you with a heartache that is unexplainable and a deep pain that hurts like no other. A child is taken up to a new and glorious life. He lives on forever, in the presence of Jesus, fully alive and happy. While those truths bring great comfort, there is still a great loss left to deal with that can seem unbearable. In the midst of pain and great sorrow, God desires to make beauty for ashes. Allowing Him to do this is a choice that those who are left behind with heavy hearts must make. As unbelievable as it initially seemed, there was a race left for ME to run after Dustin's passing. There was a new life, with Jesus, mapped out for me that was vacant in my old life. Because there was a death, ashes appeared. I had to choose what to do with those precious ashes of mine. Rather than cling to them, and allow them to cling to me, I chose to give them to Jesus. I didn't give Him all of my ashes at once; it was a gradual process that took time and cooperation. Out of those very ashes came new joy. It is a joy that cannot be taken away, and it is a joy that is worth sharing. Jesus is our beauty when we are covered in ashes, and as we relinquish our ashes to Him, His beauty shines through our lives. That's beauty for ashes.

PSALM 34:18   JAMES 4:8   PSALM 126:5–6

Prayer: I am brokenhearted, and I am crushed in spirit. I don't even know how to give You my ashes, much less to believe for them to be turned into joy. I can't imagine ever feeling true joy again amidst the great loss I feel. Holy Spirit, please help me. I need help! In the middle of this great grief, help me to draw near to You and believe Your Word. Holy Spirit, please help me to protect my heart so that bitterness doesn't find a place to take root. Please cause my tears to be a sweet healing rain for the promised season of joy to come.

90 Days of Devotions and Prayers

Day 36
Poetic Justice

Have you been lied to, cheated on, or abused?

Were you fired, not hired, or underappreciated?

Were you overlooked, slandered, or forgotten?

You have a God who never sleeps or slumbers until He brings justice to His elect.

He draws near to the brokenhearted and saves those who are crushed in spirit.

He stands with the accused and vindicates the abused.

Recommended Reading: *How to Respond When You Feel Mistreated* by John Bevere

Luke 18:6–8   Psalm 34:15–22
Psalm 35   Psalm 43:1   Psalm 57:2–3
Romans 12:19   Psalm 17

Prayer: Thank you, Father, that You are my advocate, my defender, and my righteous judge. Help me to trust You, rather than myself, to bring the justice I am due. I am hurt and angry and the temptation to take matters into my own hands is great. Help me to resist the strong desire to take revenge for how I have been wronged. Help me to forgive, love, and pray for my enemies. Help me to forgive every time the hurtful situation comes to my mind. Lead me on this higher path that few choose to follow.

Day 37
From Jealous to Zealous

While driving down the road, a random woman from my community came to mind. I've barely met this woman, and she wouldn't know me from a hole in the wall. Almost instantly, I realized that my feelings toward her were not that great, and it didn't take me long to trace the emotions back to their root cause — jealousy. Having been a Christian for decades, I am obviously aware that jealousy is not a good thing, even if no one besides me knows of its existence. As I'm processing this discovery, and how to remove the ugly root, the thought of "from jealous to zealous," popped into my heart. It seems that removing this root will require me to partner with the Holy Spirit, instead of me just passively waiting for Him to remove it for me. So, when she comes to mind, I'm going to be zealous to pray in the Spirit for her and I will zealously bless her when I am given the opportunity. I've been around the block long enough to know that when He gives a prescription for what ails you, taking the full course of His medication is not only the wise thing to do, it's the perfectly EFFECTIVE thing to do.

1 Peter 2:1–2   Psalm 139:23–24
Romans 2:4

Prayer: Holy Spirit, I give You permission to search my heart, and reveal anything in it that offends You. When You pinpoint something, help me to receive the gift of repentance. Show me the most effective way to partner with You in removing the root that You have identified. Since today's topic is jealousy, please show me if there is anyone I am envious of. If there is, please help me to put aside jealousy, and help me to grow more and more confident of who I am in You!

Day 38
Missed Season?

Does your inner flame feel too weak to get you to your finish line? Fear not. Jesus is not only the Author of your faith, but the Finisher! Release yourself from that guilt and shame. Meet your Finisher. Look up at Him, and allow Him to wash over you afresh today with His faithfulness.

Hebrews 12:2

Prayer: Holy Spirit, I am tired and weary. Instead of struggling to try to reinvigorate myself, please help me to allow You to pick me up, and carry me across the finish line.

Day 39
Save Your Energy

About a week ago, I had a phrase come to me in the night. I heard, "Save your energy for the world." I'm still pondering this one with the Lord, but I believe I have at least an initial understanding. Lately, I've found myself preoccupied with family life. Not just family life, in general, but with the "lives" of each member of my family, including my own. I've been in a "swirl" with situations that have become more and more overpowering the longer I stare at them. To be honest, hearing the phrase only made me aware of a problem I already knew existed. I just didn't realize its reach. Expending so much mental and emotional energy on my own family hasn't left much for anything else. I would love to report that I've completely shaken the concerns of my family in favor of focusing on the nations, but that would not be quite true. I know of my need for Him to overshadow my world with His, but how is that accomplished? Well, I have repented, and now I'm back to the familiar place of, "Help me, Lord." I'm also reminding myself of something my mentor has told me many times, "The lesser is included in the greater." In other words, as I save my energy for His world, He takes care of my little corner of it.

Matthew 28:18–20
Luke 24:45–47   Acts 1:8

Prayer: Holy Spirit, please help me to fully surrender my family to You. Help me to allow You to perfect the things that concern me and give me Your prayers for the nations, along with Your hope, love, compassion, and zeal for the world. Loose me from the "family ties" that bind me, and help me to bind each one, including myself, to the altar of Your love.

Day 40
Love One Another

Jesus said for us to cast our cares upon Him, and He will care for us. He lived and died for us. The question is, are we willing to do the same for others? A great service we can render to God is to do for others what Jesus did for us. One of our highest aspirations should be to follow in the footsteps of our elder brother, Jesus, by being willing to sacrifice our lives for the sake of others.

We are called unto perfection (Heb 6:1), but the whole Body of Christ can't attain to this goal unless every member is perfect. "For the body is not one member, but many" (1 Cor 12:14). Rather than judge people because of their shortcomings, we should strive for perfection, or maturity, in our own hearts so that we can help others do the same. If we have victories in our lives, we do well to remember that it's not just for our own sake, but also, to equip us to help set others free.

God also uses our prayers for others to help bring them to maturity. Moses went to God and asked Him to have mercy on His people. Esther went to the king on behalf of her people, and Joseph did the same. As ones who can go before the King of Kings and have the privilege of seeing Him face to face, we mustn't be selfish. We should present the needs of others before Him, just as the great men and women of old did. Jesus, Himself, lives to make intercession for us (Heb 7:25). Shouldn't we do the same for others?

We must lay down our lives for our friends through sacrifice and prayer so that we can help them to "mature to the full measure of the stature of Christ" (Eph 4:13 BSB). Dying to ourselves is also dying *for* others. As we do this, we play a beautiful role in helping to make the bride ready for the wedding feast of the Lamb (Rev 19:7).

Galatians 6:2   1 Corinthians 12:26
Romans 11:31

Prayer: Help me, Jesus, to put away selfishness and become more mindful of others today. Help me to overcome so that I can help others do the same. I ask You to show me how I can help my brother and sister attain to maturity in Christ, and please guide my heart as I intercede for others so that my prayers are in accordance with Your will.

Day 41
The Power of Silence

I love mornings when everything is quiet and the sun is peeking over the horizon, before all the busyness of the day begins. I sit quietly and enjoy the newness of the day, when His mercies are renewed. I say to my soul, "This is the day the LORD has made; [I] will rejoice and be glad in it" (Ps 118:24 NKJV). As I rest in the quiet, listening to God and enjoying the peace and purity of the new day, I know there is beauty and power in quietness. This type of silence is full of answers. Oh, how I cherish the mornings!

God speaks to us face to face as a friend speaks to another friend in quietness, in stillness. I'm talking about the kind of conversations that Abraham and Moses had with Him as His friends. God said to Moses that He would speak to him, meet with him, and commune with him from above the Mercy Seat in the Most Holy Place (Exod 25:22). We're passing through the busyness of the Outer Court and the Holy Place and arriving at the Most Holy Place, where all work ceases. This is a place of complete stillness with no disturbance and no agenda. From this place, we can clearly hear the voice of God speaking to us as He spoke with Moses.

Often, in my time with the Lord, I find myself speaking and speaking, or praising and worshipping, but not giving Him time to speak to me. Instead, I should stop, be silent, cease from all my works, and wait on Him. Simply enjoy basking in His presence, listening to His voice, and receiving His love. In times of busyness and great pressure, simply "Be still and know that [He is] God" (Ps 46:10).

Job 4:16   Exodus 25:22
1 Kings 19:12

Prayer: Holy Spirit, please help me to still my heart and mind and simply rest in Your presence. Help me to move past the Outer Court and the Holy Place to meet with You at the Mercy Seat. In this place, I rest in Your presence, listen to Your sweet voice, and experience the closeness of Your love.

Day 42
Father of Time

Our Father is clockwise. Entrust your days, every one of them, into the timing of His clock's hands. Trust the wisdom of God's timing for each trial, each wilderness experience, and each breakthrough. He is God of the Breakthrough, but you must also trust that He is God of the timing of your breakthrough. He has appointed times for you to enter seasons, and He has appointed times for you to exit them.

Sometimes, toward the end of a sermon, my pastor will ask, "Who will give me 5?" By now, we all know what he's asking. "Who will give me five more minutes to preach?" In the same way, I hear the Father asking, "Who will give me the latitude of five more minutes to complete this season that I began with you?" It isn't lost on me that the number five represents grace. As hard as it may be to agree to give Him five more minutes, I believe they are to be filled with "finishing graces," that are crucial to our breakthrough. There are lessons to be learned that can only be taught and caught during the last grace-filled moments of a season.

Back to my pastor. Someone is always gracious enough to raise his hand to extend the luxury of more time. But, I have a feeling that even if the congregation didn't allow more time, the pastor would extend grace to himself to finish the point He is trying to make. I believe the same is true of God and us. He knows we cannot leave this season and be successful in the next without learning the crucial lessons of grace that He has in store; they are related to "the more," that we have been asking for.

ECCLESIASTES 3:1

Prayer: Holy Spirit, please help me to take a seat at Your timetable and give myself completely to the plans that You have for me, as well as the timing of them. Help me to relax and trust that You are not unaware of how long I have been in this place of waiting and transition. Please help me to abide, in time, with You and embrace the mysteries of grace that are reserved for this place.

Day 43
God of the Breakthrough

I've heard actors refer to their first real success in "the business" as their big break. I've also heard stories of starving and discouraged actors who almost quit right before their big break. This devotion is for those who feel their faith is discouraged or on the brink of starvation.

As I write this, I am praying for you. I am praying that your faith will not fail and that the Holy Spirit will help you to look upon Jesus and follow in His enduring footsteps. This afternoon I felt the Lord wanted me to encourage you that like the Church of Philadelphia, He sees that you have kept His word, and He knows that you have little strength left (See Rev 3:7–13). His compassions toward you are great.

I also felt the Holy Spirit wanted me to encourage someone that situations you perceive as frustrating delays are actually divinely inspired, and that you should treat them as such. I ask that as you sleep tonight, the God of the Breakthrough will come alongside to energize your faith and inspire hope by whatever means necessary for your unique personality and situation. I ask Him to refresh visions, words, and dreams from the past that started you on this journey of faith. He is the Author and He is the Finisher of your faith. Be reminded that there is much at stake. I bless you with enduring strength and enabling grace to finish, in faith, and to finish well.

**Hebrews 12:2   2 Samuel 5:20
1 Chronicles 14:11   Luke 18:8   Luke 22:32**

Prayer: Holy Spirit, right now, at this stage in my journey, please help me to look unto Jesus, the Author and Finisher of my faith, and help me to follow in His footsteps. Help me to endure hardship for the joy that is set before me. Help me to know and believe that there is an end to this season and that there truly is joy set before me. Help me to not grow discouraged, disenfranchised, or angry with You, my best friend, because of weariness and discouragement. When I perceive yet another delay of entrance into my personal "promised land," help me to settle down and, by faith, believe that the delays are truly divine. Please encourage me out of my discouragement.

Day 44
The Master Gardener

Allow My pruning, for I am gentle. I do it out of complete love for you. When pruning is taking place, the plant looks as if it is being defeated, cut off, and left to die, but that is not true. Also, remember that thorns hurt when they are being removed. However, what a relief to no longer live with thorns but to have true healing, true freedom. Now the flowers and fruit can come forth!

Isaiah 30:18-21   John 15:1-8

Prayer: Holy Spirit, please help me to be still during the pruning process, to accept the shears and the lessons they carry. Help me to cooperate with You in removing those things that are not needed and in shaping things that need adjusting. Remind me that the shears are held by the most loving and capable hands in the world and that while You are doing your careful work, I can listen for the sound of the turtledove, anticipating that the figs are about to be brought forth and the flowers are about to bloom. Thank You that shearing season means that Spring is in the air (Song 2).

Day 45
Going Through

We have to go THROUGH the dark parts and THROUGH the hard parts to get to the good parts, which will end up being the best parts.

Psalm 23

Prayer: Holy Spirit, please help me to go through, all the way through, with You! Help me to have real hope that the best is yet to come and that it is worth contending for.

DAY 46
Give Way

Coming out of the cocoon is a painful process, but the beauty and light that awaits on the other side of the cramped living quarters is both breathtaking and worth the struggle. You have endured cocooning; it is time to "give way" to the emerging process. Giving way is the moment at which breaking through begins. Breakthrough will look and feel like the culmination of all the time you have spent in the cocoon. It's a time of great challenges being launched your way, but the Lord would have you know that there is no need to be afraid of the challenges you are facing. He is the fourth man in the fire with you. He would also have you know that breakthrough is designed to be a short season, especially in comparison to cocooning. It's intense, but it's meant to be short-lived. You do have a choice in the matter. You can resist breakthrough and cause what is meant to be a short season to linger, or you can return to the relative comfort and familiarity of the cocoon. Make no mistake, there is no escaping the breakthrough process of the equation if you are to ever complete the metamorphosis and emerge a beautiful butterfly. If you refuse it now, it will circle back later. Remember, you are not alone, and He will not bring you to the point of breakthrough if you aren't equipped to handle it by His grace, because grace gives way to glory. Just as He was with you in the cocoon, He is with you in the breakthrough. He has moved from beside you to in front of you as your Breaker. Once you have fully emerged from the cocoon, there will be no going back, and you will come forth as pure gold. And then, you will share your breakthrough story with others who need coaxing out of their own cocoons.

MICAH 2:13   DANIEL 3   PSALM 46:5
ISAIAH 66:9   JOB 23:10   1 PETER 1:7

Prayer: Holy Spirit, Please HELP ME! Help me to trust You and Your faith in my ability to handle the breakthrough process at this moment in time. Help me to traverse this place as quickly as possible, refusing to go back to the cocoon or to prolong my time of breakthrough through "negotiations" or "hemming and hawing." Help me to fully surrender to the breakthrough process. Remind me that I am not surrendering to just anyone or anything. I am surrendering to You, to pure love. Heaven help me!

Day 47
Heavenly Raiment

Your trials are clothing you with garments to be worn in life everlasting.

James 1:12   1 Peter 1:6
Revelation 12:11

Prayer: Holy Spirit, rather than trying to desperately shrug off the trials I have been given "to wear," help me wear them an as opportunist, trusting that the testing of my faith produces endurance. Help me to "let endurance have its perfect result, so that [I] may be perfect and complete, lacking in nothing" (Jas 1:4 NASB).

Day 48
Faith

You ask for faith to move mountains. I want to give you faith to move nations and generations!

Matthew 17:20   Psalm 2:8

Prayer: Holy Spirit, please enlarge my faith beyond asking for the mountains in my own life to be removed. Give me a heart for the nations and for the generations that are coming behind me.

Day 49
Guiding Eye

"I will instruct you and teach you in the way you should go;
I will guide you with My eye" (Ps 32:8 NKJV).

The Lord has often spoken to me through this verse, and He has given me a beautiful visual to demonstrate its power and tenderness. I think of a mother watching her young child, making sure the child doesn't wander too far or go near anything unsafe. She watches with such loving concern, not in anger or strictness, but in a way that makes the child feel safe and secure. I believe our Heavenly Father keeps His eye upon us in just the same way.

2 Chronicles 16:9   Genesis 28:15 (Amp)

Prayer: Holy Spirit, please help me to believe that You are intimately acquainted with all my ways and that You desire to show me the best choices and direction for my life. Help me to trust Your guiding eye and to learn to perceive the instructions and guidance that You are giving.

Day 50
Crosshairs: A Person of Interest

Do you ever have the feeling that the enemy has you in his crosshairs, that you are a target of his interests, and that every weapon formed against you is coming dangerously close to hitting its intended mark? When seasons are "hot," run to the solace of the cross. The cross is your home base, and you are declared safe beneath the shelter of His wings. Hide in the safety of the cross that cries, "It is finished; rest, My child!" As you rest in Him, when He moves, you move. This divine movement intercepts the enemy's attack and keeps you safe from all weapons formed against you. Because you are a person of interest, you will find yourself in the enemy's crosshairs. Remember the One who has each of your hairs numbered and remember to remain hidden in His cross.

Psalm 91   Isaiah 54:17   Psalm 68:13

Prayer: Holy Spirit, I am feeling overwhelmed by the trials I'm facing. It feels like so many weapons have been launched against me, and I don't know what to do about many of them. Please help me to remember that You have "finished" each of these trails, and help me to rest in that knowledge. Cause the knowledge to move from my head to my heart, so that I can truly rest in the finished work of the cross.

Day 51
Edge of Glory

God is on the edge of His throne with liquid gold flowing, in abundance, out of His hands. It is anointing for anyone who is willing to open his mouth and speak on the Lord's behalf. He is right on the edge of pouring out His Spirit upon all flesh. It will be the greatest revival the world has ever seen.

Acts 2:17–21   Psalm 45:1
Zechariah 4:11–14

Prayer: Holy Spirit, Thank you for your precious anointing oil. Help me to open my mouth to receive Your words. Give me a heart that not only receives your words but obediently releases them. Thank You for revival. I pray that You would send workers into the field to gather the harvest (Matt 9:38).

Day 52
Hide

"Keep me as the apple of your eye; hide me in the shadow of your wings, from the wicked who do me violence, my deadly enemies who surround me" (Ps 17:8–9 ESV).

As a child, I always felt safest when I rolled up in a ball in bed with my eyes closed and a blanket covering me. Sometimes, I would peek out over the blanket to see if it was safe to come out. As an adult, this trick didn't work any longer and anxiety and worry consumed my life, day and night. At 30, I was a chronic insomniac and illness resulted from the lack of sleep. After reading Psalm 17: 8–9, I envisioned myself hiding under the pinions of the Most High, peeking through the feathers to see if it was okay to come out. This gave me such a warm and safe feeling, even better than the bed and blanket did when I was a child. Knowing He covers me with His mighty wings has broken through the insomnia, and anxiety no longer has a hold over me. Praise be to God!

Isaiah 26:20   Psalm 61:3

Prayer: Holy Spirit, please help me to see myself as the apple of Your eye. As the apple of Your eye, help me to be willing to stay hidden in the shadow of Your wings until You tell me it's safe to come out from hiding.

Day 53
Truth

Truth is for tearing down and building up: Tearing down strongholds and building people up.

1 John 3:18   2 Corinthians 10:4

Prayer: Holy Spirit, please fit my heart and my mouth with truth — truth for tearing down and truth for building up. Help me to express truth in the way that is best fitted to the hearer's ear and heart.

Day 54

Surrender

Question: How does God create something from nothing?

Answer: When we give Him ourselves.

We are the created, and He's the Creator of all things. When we submit ourselves to Him, He starts a lifelong work of creating something of value and beauty. He takes our ashes and creates a masterpiece to be put on display for the world to see. When we surrender, we become a blank canvas. We empty ourselves of all of US to be filled with all of HIM. This "art of surrender" allows Him the freedom to do His best and most complete work in our lives. The most beautiful picture in the world is of a completely surrendered people, willing to be put on display for the glory of the Master Artist!

Philippians 1:6   Isaiah 64:8
Isaiah 61:3

Prayer: Help me, Father, to keep surrendering, even when it hurts. Just as Jesus surrendered His life for me, for love's sake, help me to surrender my all to You, for love's sake.

Day 55
Gathering Grace

Gathering grace is a current event. There is grace sufficient for THIS day. When you attempt to gather grace for some future day or event, you frustrate the grace of God that is provided for today. While trying to gather for a future date, you bypass what has been provided for today, and thus, you begin to doubt that grace will be provided for your harrowing tomorrows. Train your senses and your soul to focus only on what is on your plate for today, and receive the grace afforded for the current events of your life — today's events. Worrying about whether or not grace will be available for two weeks from now, or trying to figure out what form it will take, blinds you to the beautiful grace that is provided for today. Once you train yourself in this manner, you will realize there is no need to store up grace for the coming days because He's always faithful to provide what is needed for the current day's events.

Exodus 16:18   2 Corinthians 8:15
2 Corinthians 12:9

Prayer: Holy Spirit, please help me to discipline and train myself to only look at the present day that I am living in. Help me to gather grace for this morning and grow my faith to be able to release tomorrow's cares into Your keeping. Just as the Israelites were instructed to gather manna morning by morning, help me to gather mercy for each day. Help me to trust that You will provide for my tomorrows without me trying to understand, in advance, how You will choose to provide.

Day 56
The Pause

Many mistakes and regrets can be avoided by practicing "the art of the pause." You learn this art through practice. Practice pausing before responding, before accepting engagements, or making commitments. Don't just pause; pause with Me and you will transition beautifully into the fertile season that I am bringing you into. It is a weighty season; heavy laden with gifts to be opened within you and shared with the world around you. Pause to anticipate what is to come with Me. Great discoveries and surprises are ahead! Selah — Pause calmly and think about that.

James 1:19   Isaiah 30:21

Prayer: Holy Spirit, please help me to discipline myself to pause with You before I make commitments for my time. Help me to not be fearful of telling people that I'll have to get back to them with an answer.

DAY 57
Mistakes

"Make room for mistakes." Several years ago, I heard that simple, but powerful, statement in the middle of the night. My personal definition of a "mistake" is when you make what turns out to be a bad decision with the best of intentions. It's not deliberately sinning. For people who lean toward perfectionism, making a simple mistake can be heart-wrenching and cause much wallowing in guilt, regret, and condemnation. In your spiritual life, if you're going to make progress, there will be risks involved. Some risks work out as hoped, and others will be mistakes. Not only have "all sinned and fallen short of the glory of God," but all have made mistakes and fallen short of the glory of God. Release yourself from the guilt and regret of former mistakes, and watch for God to bring beauty from them, even if it's simply in the form of lessons learned for yourself and for those who come after you.

Romans 8:1   Romans 8:28   Romans 3:23

Prayer: Holy Spirit, please help me to not be paralyzed by indecision for the fear of making a mistake. When I do make mistakes, help me to learn from them and release myself from regret and condemnation. Ultimately, help me to trust that even my "well-meaning mistakes" are a part of the beautiful tapestry that You are weaving into my life.

Day 58
Whose Meal Will It Be?

When the devil speaks, you have two choices:

- A. Eat his words.
- B. Make him eat his words.

Regardless of how enticing or truthful his voice may be, there is a Plan B. Choose it!

1 Peter 5:8–9   **John 10:10**
Ephesians 4:27   **Proverbs 18:21**

Prayer: Holy Spirit, please give me the ability to discern between truth and lies, especially if the lies are laced with enough truth to make them plausible. When lies are spoken to my heart, help me to lift up the shield of faith to extinguish the flaming arrows of the devil. Please give me truth to speak to myself that combats the lies and causes the devil to flee from me (Eph 6:16 and Jas 4:7).

DAY 59
Second Chances

This morning, a friend of mine texted me a portion of a book that she's reading. It was all about not dwelling on the past. You see, this dear friend has made some choices in life that she knew were not good at the time she was making them. She was strongly advised not to continue on the path that she was on, but she didn't listen. As a result, her family was broken up and there has been a lot of fall out for her to deal with. The biggest struggle my friend has had is believing that God could possibly have anything good in store for her, even though she has genuinely repented.

My response to her this morning:

"I really believe that correctly handling the sin of our past is a steppingstone to our future. Most will take one of two tracks: (1) They figure they've already messed up their life, so "the heck with it" and they continue down the path of mistake after mistake after mistake; (2) They are deeply sorry for what they have done, ask God to forgive them and maybe receive the forgiveness in their heads, but not in their hearts. As a result, they keep wallowing around in shame and regret, refusing to believe God still has a good plan for them."

If you find yourself in a similar situation of shame and regret, my advice to you is what I spoke to my friend this morning. "You will be one of the few to take the 3rd track. Yes, you (like all of us) have sinned and fallen short of the glory of God. But you also have the provision of forgiveness that Jesus bought for you on the cross so that you can look forward to, and participate with, the good plan that God has in store for you. In the end, even the poor choices in life that you have made, repented of, and released, will serve to speak of the goodness of God and His unfailing love and mercy."

1 John 1:9   Micah 7:19   Philippians 3:13–14
2 Corinthians 5:17   Isaiah 43:18–19

Prayer: Father, You and I both know I have doubted that You truly have a good plan for my life because of the horrible mistakes and choices that I have made. Please forgive me for my unbelieving heart, for doubting Your goodness and grace. Please help me to leave my past behind, with all of its failures, and help me to believe that You have a good future in store for me. Please give me a glimpse of what You see in my future so that I have something lovely to aspire toward (Phil 4:8).

Day 60
Happy Birthday

Spend some time in the Psalms today. Choose the psalms you read based on your birthday. For example, if your birthday is 12–2–52, read and meditate on Psalm 12, Psalm 2, and Psalm 52. Allow what you read to minister to you, and receive the words as gifts for the day. If today happens to be your actual birthday, "Happy Birthday, with much love!" If not, go ahead and pretend like it is, and spend your day celebrating the gift of life you have been given!

Acts 17:11   1 Corinthians 2:9

A Birthday Blessing/Prayer for your year: Like the Bereans, as you examine the Scriptures, may you receive their messages eagerly and may your eyes be opened in childlike wonder to the mysteries that are prepared to unfold before you. May you become rooted and grounded in the love of God more fully than any other year in your life, and may you share His love in tangible ways with the world around you.

Day 61
By Faith, Dress in Hope

Dress for the weather you prayed for, not what the weatherman reported.

2 Corinthians 4:18   Hebrews 11:1

Prayer: Father, regardless of what my life's current "weather conditions" forecast, please help me, by faith, to dress in the hope that "I will see the goodness of the LORD in the land of the living" (Ps 27:13 NIV).

Day 62
A Pure Heart

God is honored in our asking when the asking is from a pure heart. What's your motive?

1 Kings 3:10–14   Proverbs 4:23

Prayer: Holy Spirit, You are well aware of the prayers I have been praying. You know my heart in these requests better than I do. I give You permission to search my heart and show me if I am praying out of anything other than a pure heart. If there are traces of self-ambition, or any other motive that is less than pure, please show me, and help me to turn from my evil ways. Then, please lead me in the everlasting way, and help me to follow (Ps 139:23–24).

Day 63
Goodness Gracious

I'm from the Deep South. Recently I heard an old saying, and my spirit came to attention within me. The saying is "goodness gracious." Because I've been focusing so much on the grace and mercy of God, I have a newfound appreciation for this phrase from my childhood. Where I'm from, we would use the saying to respond to a surprising statement, whether the subject matter was surprisingly good or surprisingly bad.

May God's grace and goodness be poured into your life in full measure so that you ooze these beautiful attributes everywhere you go, transforming people and places from bad to good and from good to better. Take the time to be transformed in His presence today so that you may be a transformer as you go along your way. His goodness is indeed gracious!

2 Corinthians 3:18

Prayer: Holy Spirit, as I sit with You today, please cause me to be conformed into the beauty of your glorious image so that everywhere I go, people, places, and situations are impacted and transformed by the goodness of Your grace.

Day 64
Cucumbers, Anyone?

I just received a group text from one of my friends asking if any of us would like cucumbers from her garden. In commenting on the size of some of her cucumbers, she made the following statement: "We had some jumbo cucumbers hidden under leaves and vines. They've had more time for growing extra-large. There's an object lesson here. Don't let our season of "hiddenness," though it seems to go on and on, be discouraging. We are hidden for a season for a reason — growth!" She continued, "The Lord spoke to me a long time ago when I was picking blueberries. He said that sometimes the largest and sweetest blueberries are hidden in places that are a bit harder to get to." A few "cucumber texts" ensued, inspired by our friend's original text. One "big cucumber" concern was that the bigger cucumbers lose their sweetness. Another friend made this observation. Big cucumbers are mostly seeds, but this is good for replanting (multiplication) for the following season. My farmer friend ended her text with the following: "Let us stay hidden under the shadow of the Almighty. He will showcase us, His bride, in His time. Our cucumbers, both large and small, are sweet. They are some of the best cucumbers I've ever had! If we allow God to do His perfect work in us, we will remain very sweet and full of seeds for a future harvest."

Ecclesiastes 3:11   Psalm 75:6–7
1 Peter 5:6–7   Psalm 91:1–2

Prayer: Holy Spirit, You know better than me the plans that You have for my life. But, I am so excited about the parts of my life's puzzle that You have revealed! In my zeal to be all that You have called me to be, please help me to remain hidden within the School of the Spirit until it is time for Your plans to manifest in my life. Help me to trust Your timing because promotion comes from You, not through self-effort.

Day 65
Fruit Medley

This morning, the old phrase, "dressed to the nines," came to mind. Immediately, I thought of being dressed in the fruit of the Holy Spirit because His fruit consists of nine attributes: love, joy, peace, patience, kindness, goodness, gentleness, faithfulness, and self-control. It's not nine different pieces of fruit; it's one fruit with each of these beautiful descriptives on display. Think of a grape. It's one fruit, but it can be purple, sweet, tart, and snappy all at the same time. As we give ourselves to the guidance of the Holy Spirit, we can expect our lives to become a well-rounded display of His fruit, a beautiful fruit medley for the world to taste and see, and ultimately know, that He is God.

Galatians 5:22–23   Ephesians 6:17–18

Prayer: Dear Holy Spirit, please help me to become more intimately aware of Your presence inside of me. Help me to fellowship with You and learn Your likes and dislikes so that I can adapt my behavior to parallel Who You are. Even when my life feels like a fruit basket that has been turned over by adverse circumstances, cause my life to become a beautiful display of love, joy, peace, patience, kindness, goodness, gentleness, and self-control.

Day 66
Cloud of Witnesses

More and more, I am aware of the vastness of what Jesus purchased for us on the cross. Yes, He purchased our salvation, and how great a salvation it is! However, our "benefit package" doesn't stop there. Psalm 103:2 says that we should "bless the LORD, O my soul, and forget not ALL his benefits" (emphasis added). One benefit that tends to be overlooked is the cloud of witnesses. These saints are missed on earth, but their presence in Heaven is to our benefit! After a close friend of mine died, the Lord showed me that she and I are on two sides of the same team. Her prayers, which have the advantage of Heaven's perspective, are mixed with mine, and this is a powerful combination! During that same season, I felt the Lord ask me to pray for something unconventional. One day, I sensed Him prompting me to ask for specific members of the cloud of witnesses to pray for me. Each person, including my Mama, is someone very special in my life. After praying, I asked the Lord to provide some sort of confirmation for the unusual prayer request. Later, the same day, I was dusting some bookshelves in my den and came across a book that had belonged to my Mama (incidentally, Mama's first name was Jewel). The name of the book is *Cloudy Jewel*, by Grace Livingston. If you have lost loved ones, remember they aren't lost at all. They are a part of the great cloud of witnesses, praying for you and cheering you on as you complete the race that is set before you. These beloved saints are healthy and active in their eternal home, and they partner with us, in prayer, for things that concern us as well as the kingdom of Heaven.

Recommended Reading: *Intra Muros* by Rebecca Ruter Springer

Hebrews 12:1–3

Prayer: Father, I thank You that You have given me such a large "benefits package." I am sure it is much larger than my "religious background" has framed for me, so please knock down any unintended walls and expand my heart to include every benefit that You purchased for me through Jesus' death on the cross. Thank You for the cloud of witnesses and the important role they play; please show me how to partner with them to see Your kingdom come upon the earth in ways I have never imagined.

Day 67
If You Complain, You Remain

Last week I was on speaker phone with a friend. Her teenage son walked into the room and said, "Hi," to me. I said, "Hey Luke, how are you doing?" His reply: "I can't complain." To him, it was just a reply. To me, it felt like Luke's voice was a bullhorn issuing a strong directive from the Lord, "You cannot, you must not complain." Later, the same day, I overheard two men greet each other. One man said to the other, "How are you?" He responded, "I can't complain." Honestly, I heard the message loud and clear the first time it came, but this second rendition sealed the deal. I know that murmuring and complaining is never a good thing, but for this particular season, it seems even more imperative that I speak words of Spirit and life! As you go about your way, let your words be filled with life, and may they grow sweeter and sweeter day by day!

Numbers 11   Philippians 2:14
Romans 14:19

Prayer: Holy Spirit, please help me to speak Your life-giving words today. If I begin to release a word that is not in another's best interest, please prick my heart, and help me to heed Your voice and keep my mouth shut. Furthermore, please replace the words of death that I planned to release with life-giving words of Your choosing.

Day 68
Heart Murmur

Years ago, while I was spending time with the Lord, five words rose up in my spirit. I didn't hear an audible voice, but it might as well have been. The strong statement was, "You have a heart murmur." There was no argument to be had. The statement was a play on words. As a child, I had been diagnosed with a heart murmur, and I vaguely remember making yearly trips to the city to have my heart condition checked. However, the morning the "heart murmur" word came, I knew the Lord wasn't referring to the physical condition of my heart, but the spiritual one. I knew better than to argue. I asked for forgiveness. I asked for help in keeping my heart with all diligence because it is out of the heart that the mouth speaks (Prov 4:23 and Luke 6:45). The Bible says, in the Book of James, that no man can tame the tongue, but, fortunately, we have an excellent "tamer" living within us. It's the Holy Spirit. We have but to ask Him, and He will gladly prick our hearts before we speak any words better left unsaid. Our Master Craftsman is not content to work on surface issues (our words); He's much more interested in the heart of the matter. If we allow Him, He will be faithful to trace our negative words back to their roots, which are anchored in our hearts. When our heart issues are resolved, life-giving words will issue from our mouths much more easily, even in trying circumstances.

Psalm 51:10   Philippians 2:14
Exodus 15:22–25   Exodus 16:1–2

Prayer: Holy Spirit, please search my heart and show me if there is any wicked way in me that would eventually find its way to and through my mouth. Help me to agree with You and repent, instead of becoming defensive. Please fill those places with Your love, grace, and mercy so that my words are pleasing to You and a blessing to those who hear them.

DAY 69
The Spoken Word

Several years ago, the Holy Spirit spoke the following statement to my heart: "Angels ride on our words." For as long as I can remember, I have known the creative power of words. After all, we are created in the image of God, and He created the heavens and the earth through the power of His spoken word. However, hearing this statement added fuel to my fire. It spurred me to not just watch over my mouth so that I don't speak negative words, but to actively speak life-giving words (His words). Then, angels will echo those life-giving words into the spirit realm. If you are at a loss as to where to begin, you need look no further than the Word of God. The Bible is packed with words you can personalize and speak over yourself. For example: "[I] always rejoice; [I] pray without ceasing. In everything [I] give thanks; for this is God's will for [me] in Christ Jesus. [I] do not quench the Spirit, and [I] do not despise prophetic utterances" (1 Thess 5:16–22 NASB). Prophetic utterances are another great source for making decrees for angels to ride on. Dust off those words that the Lord has given to you over the decades and release them into the atmosphere so that the angels can ride on them. Let's give angels something good to talk about! They are available and waiting to help us!

PSALM 103:20   HEBREWS 1:14
ROMANS 4:17

Prayer: Heavenly Father, thank You so much for the ministry of angels in my life. In addition to giving them effective words to ride on, please show me how to best partner with angels in my everyday life. Open my heart and mind to receive all the help that is available to me from Your heavenly hosts.

Day 70

Song of Solomon 2

Have you been going through a particularly hard season? Maybe your whole year, or decade, could be characterized that way. If this is you, remember that "the LORD is near to the brokenhearted and saves those who are crushed in spirit" (Ps 34:18 NASB). Take advantage of His nearness. Put pen to paper and pour your heart upon the One Who longs to hear your voice. Listen carefully, and you will hear the voice of your Bridegroom calling back to you. Record all the thoughts that pour from your heart. Then, take time to sit still and listen for the voice of your Beloved. Ask Him what He would like to say to you and then just listen. He will be faithful to respond. Record the thoughts that come to you from His heart. You will find that His thoughts toward you are only good.

I bless you, my sweet friend. May you receive the love and comfort of the Holy Spirit to carry you through this season in your life. He is doing a new thing, and He would have you to be aware of it (Isa 43:19).

Recommended Reading: *How to Hear God's Voice*, by Mark Virkler

Jeremiah 33:3

Prayer from my heart for yours: Father, I pray that You would help my friend pour her heart out to You, and I ask that You would whisper words of love, encouragement, and affection back to her. Open her ears to hear and her heart to receive what You long to say to her.

Day 71
One Thing

One thing I desire. One thing I desire is You, Lord.

I can no longer live outside of Your love. Lord, I cannot even contemplate what it would be like to live outside of Your love. How would I breathe? Who would I trust? How could I possibly live outside of You? For You are my life. My longing is for You and You alone. I know that You are mine, and I am most certainly Yours, for who else would I belong to if not You? Who would I love? Who would I long to spend unending time with, and who would I continuously be seeking to get alone with? Whose voice would I listen for, and whose words of love would move my heart as Yours? Who, other than You, would I confess my love to and set my affections upon? Who would love me with the same pure love that You have in Your heart for me? On whom would I fix my desire? I long to worship and reach out and touch You with gentleness and warmth of spirit, knowing that You reach out to me with the same longing desire. On whom would my thoughts land and ponder, if not You?

Who else, but You, would wipe my tears, lift my head, and hold my hand? Who would know my every need before even I know it? Who else would fulfill my every desire and satisfy me in such a deep and beautiful way that I have no wants, other than more, more of You? You are the One I can never get enough of. My soul looks for You everywhere and in everything. My mind takes its greatest delight in the ever present thoughts of You; I continuously wonder about You.

You created me from dust, and to dust shall I return. But this love, this love I have, this love we share will live on. This unending love will live on for as long as love exists.

Psalm 27:4   Psalm 73:25–26

Prayer: Holy Spirit, please maintain my cause of loving You supremely all the days of my life. I don't want this to be a fleeting season, but the mainstay of my life until I am joined with You in Heaven's eternity.

Day 72

Eyes to See

Have you ever had a day when you felt out of it? I think we all experience that feeling from time to time. When I sense those emotions, I've learned to go outside into nature. There's something captivating about the fresh air, the gentle breeze, the blue sky, and the puffy, white clouds. It lifts your spirit and brings joy to your heart. It's interesting to think that the first man and woman were created to live in a garden, outside in nature and surrounded by beauty. Wouldn't it be wonderful if we still lived in that garden? I remember once sensing what a "little piece of Heaven" must be like. I was at a beautiful park, walking on a winding trail, surrounded by a lush canopy of trees. The air was fresh, and the birds were singing. The trail opened up to a beautiful lake that was surrounded by a hill of gorgeous flowers that were cascading down the slope. The scene before me looked like a rainbow of vivid color! The sun danced off the water, making the lily pads look like they were floating among glistening diamonds. The glory of the Lord was unfolding before my eyes. It felt as if I was receiving a bouquet from Heaven, a kiss from the Lord! I sat there and drank it in, alone with my Creator. There are no colors as spectacular as the colors of nature created by the hand of the Lord. We are surrounded by a beautiful display of God's craftsmanship and beauty. The heavens declare it, and the sky proclaims it. Take time, today, to drink in the beauty of nature, and thank Him for the beautiful gift of life and refreshment. To God be the glory!

Psalm 19:1–6

Prayer: Heavenly Father, thank You for the beauty of nature and the glory that it proclaims. Remind me to take advantage of the outdoors to lift my spirit and refresh my soul. Help me to see Your glory in the things that You have created and cause my heart to erupt in praise at the beauty of Your creativity and workmanship. Just as Adam and Eve communed with you in the garden, help me to fellowship with You in the simple act of admiring Your creation.

Day 73

Yuck, Lukewarm!

Time to eat! Imagine you're in your favorite restaurant, and you just ordered the house special. You're anxiously waiting for your server to deliver your meal. You can smell the aroma, and you can almost taste the anticipated dish. Finally, it arrives at the table, and you take your first bite, only to find it's lukewarm — yuck! Suddenly, your much anticipated meal has lost its special appeal.

Just like that disappointing meal, we, too, can become lukewarm. Revelation 3:15–17 (NASB) says, "I know your deeds, that you are neither cold nor hot; I wish that you were cold or hot. So because you are lukewarm, and neither hot nor cold, I will vomit you out of My mouth. Because you say, 'I am rich, and have become wealthy, and have no need of anything,' and you do not know that you are wretched, miserable, poor, blind, and naked." YIKES! This verse is speaking to the believers in the Laodicean Church. The people were going to church, praying and fellowshiping, but they had become complacent, indifferent, and compromised in their ways. They were going through the motions and yet they had lost their passion and zeal for the Lord. They had become spiritually bankrupt! The enemy is very subtle and sly. Remember, it's the little foxes that ruin the vines. Losing our focus, excusing sin, and pleasing people, rather than the Lord, draws us into paths that lead to compromise and spiritual blindness — lukewarmness! We must remain vigilant and on guard against the schemes of the enemy. Our Father is calling out to each of us to come closer to Him. As we seek Him first, stay in His Word, and remain steadfast in our walk, the fire in our hearts will burn stronger and stronger, hotter and hotter!

Matthew 22:37   2 Chronicles 16:9
Song of Solomon 2:15

Prayer: Fan the flame of my heart, Lord, and let me burn with passion for You. Holy Spirit, help me to hear the call to intimacy, and help me to answer the call.

DAY 74
The Power of Words

"If you can't say something nice, say nothing at all," is something my mother always said. One of the smallest members of our body, the tongue, has the power to minister life or death to others. If someone secretly attached a recorder to you for an entire day, would you be surprised at the words that were played back? Do your words build others up or tear them down? Do your words build YOURSELF up or tear YOURSELF down?

**"Set a watch, O LORD, before my mouth;
keep the door of my lips"** (Ps 141:3).

We see from the above verse that David recognized his human weakness, as well as the power of his speech. That recognition caused him to cry out to the Lord for help. It has been estimated that the average person opens his mouth to speak 700 times a day. That's a lot of words that have a profound impact on others and ourselves.

When Jesus was persecuted and slandered, He remained silent before His accusers. He is our example, and the Bible tells us that "neither was guile found in his mouth" (1 Pet 2:22). Each day holds many opportunities for us to overcome so that no guile is found in our mouths. These opportunities are allowed by the Lord to help us in our personal growth in taming our tongues. Knowledge of the Word of God is essential in our lives, but that knowledge, alone, is not a mark of spirituality. We must incorporate the Word into our daily lives. The words we speak, the decisions we make, and what we do behind closed doors are true indicators of our spiritual maturity.

Each day we should ask ourselves, "Who am I reflecting in word and in deed?" Who we reflect is a choice. May we choose well today!

Proverbs 16:24   Proverbs 18:21
James 3:2-12   Matthew 15:18

Prayer: Holy Spirit, please help me to speak and act in a manner that reflects YOU and Your glory. Cause my speech to be seasoned with grace, and "Let the words of my mouth, and the meditation of my heart, be acceptable in thy sight, O LORD, my strength, and my redeemer" (Col 4:6 and Ps 19:14). Thank you, Holy Spirit, that You are the Doorman of my mouth. When You say, "Halt," please help me to heed Your command and withdraw the words that were about to escape from the doors of my mouth.

Day 75
Drink Your Milk

Several years ago, our two-year-old Shih-tzu presented us with three little pups. All the pups were lively and healthy. Over the next several days, I watched those pups consistently nurse with an insatiable appetite for milk. After a few weeks, their eyes opened, and they graduated to soft food. They got stronger and eventually stood, took their first steps, and began to run. Watching those pups eat and grow brought to mind 1 Corinthians 3:2 (NASB), "I gave you milk to drink, not solid food; for you were not yet able to consume it." As new Christians, the Lord feeds us with the milk of His Word. As we grow in His ways and get stronger, we desire the deeper things of the Lord. He creates a greater appetite in our soul, wooing and calling us ever closer. Just as those pups ate a balanced diet on their way to maturity, we need to partake of a balanced diet of His Word daily. As we consistently drink and then move onto solid food, we will grow in His ways and reflect His glory. He will never leave us nor forsake us, always leading us onward in the journey of life and maturity in Him.

Matthew 4:4

Prayer: Holy Spirit, please help me to be as consistent in eating and drinking Your Word as those little pups were in receiving nourishment from their mother. Cause me to remain hungry so that I return to Your Word day after day, year after year, and help me to never stop maturing in You.

Day 76
Crowning Moment

Who would deny that the crowning moment in Jesus' life was the Cross, the place of victory?

He wished there was another way to accomplish His life's ultimate purpose.

> Yes, He taught.
> Yes, He healed.
> Yes, He cast out demons.
> Yes, He raised the dead.

But the crowning moment was the cross, where love and suffering met. He humbled Himself and became of no reputation for others.

Do we love others enough to suffer so that they may not?

Luke 22:42   Philippians 2:8
Philippians 3:10–11

Prayer: Holy Spirit, help me to follow in the steps of my elder brother, Jesus, so that His crowning moment becomes mine.

Day 77
Vessels of Honor

A while back, a friend brought me three vases and asked me to place floral arrangements in each one. She requested white flowers for all. As I arranged them, I noticed that the different vases seemed to call for different arrangements. One arrangement was loose and flowing, one orderly and compact, and the third was somewhere in between. It occurred to me that each of us is a vase, a vessel of honor.

Each of us calls for, requires, a different arrangement.
Each beautiful in her own way, but each unique.
Too many times we want to look at someone else.
Someone's arrangement is prettier than ours.
God made no mistake when He arranged you.
And He is still working on the arrangement.

2 Timothy 2:20–21   Psalm 139:14
Isaiah 64:8

Prayer: Heavenly Father, help me to appreciate the vessel that You have made me to be. Help me to trust that You know best how to arrange me and help me fall so in love with Your workmanship that I would not even think to compare myself to another.

Day 78
Believe and Determine

Beliefs have consequences.

Determine to believe God's words. Every one.

Mark 9:23–24

Prayer: Holy Spirit, please cause the result of my beliefs to be that I see the glory of God made manifest in the earth today.

Day 79
It's All Good, Really?

Did you know statistics show that by the age of 45, 33% of women have had an abortion? Maybe you, yourself, made the difficult decision to end a pregnancy. At the time, it felt like the right decision. Maybe you felt you were too young, too broke, or that the man who got you pregnant wasn't working out. Whatever the reason, the abortion happened, and you went on with your life. You go to work every day. You eat, sleep, and smile like everyone else. But sometimes, when you stop and acknowledge your feelings, you are confused, empty, or isolated, just to name a few of the feelings lying beneath the surface.

Here's some good news! There is a way to find complete peace and the ability to forgive. Maybe the person you need to forgive the most is yourself! Jesus is with you, and He's waiting to be your comfort and your help. Call on Him, and He will give you His forgiveness and perfect peace. Jesus' unconditional love is there for all who cry out to Him. He longs for us to rely on Him for freedom from the pain and hurt. In Him, you can find forgiveness and hope for a joyful future. There are many women who will come alongside you as you start your journey, free from the shackles of guilt and shame. Reach out to Christ and reach out to others. The day will come when you will be able to say, "It's all good," and it REALLY is!

Acts 3:19

Prayer: Father, I know in my head that Jesus was, is, and will forever be Your plan for redemption. But in my heart there is this one thing, that if I were honest, I feel is beyond Your forgiveness. And yet, I know that would mean that Jesus' death wasn't enough. I know that's not true, but my soul struggles so much. Please help me to receive the fullness of your redemption plan for every area of my life, including this very painful one. Help me to release the sin and the hurt to You, and help me to receive Your healing hand.

Day 80

In Your Eyes

Once again, Lord, I am at Your feet desiring to pour myself out before You, to lavish You with thanksgiving that becomes praise and praise that becomes worship. The sweet and intoxicating aroma of worship is what my heart longs to offer You. And yet, all that seems to pour forth is the foul stench of my own self-pity. I find myself clothed in rags, wrapped in old grave clothes that I know YOU haven't given me to wear. I have clothed myself with these lesser garments. Even in my deepest moments of despair, I realize these rags no longer fit and that they have no place in my closet. As I look into Your eyes, the grave clothes no longer hold me bound; they melt away as I look at my true reflection in Your eyes. Only in Your eyes can I find an accurate reflection of myself. As I continue to hold Your gaze, I see the woman You dreamed of when You created me. I begin to envision my proper attire with the robe of righteousness about my shoulders hanging brightly to the floor, scented with the fragrance of adoration. Now I see myself as YOU created me, free and adorned in a glorious gown, pure and brilliant, custom made, elegant in its simplistic beauty. This is who I am and how I am adorned in Your eyes, Your most beautiful eyes.

Psalm 45:13–15

Prayer: Holy Spirit, when my vision is blurred and distorted, help me to stop and stare into Your eyes. Help me to hold Your gaze until my vision is restored to Your vision.

Day 81

Warpath

Count on it, there will be seasons in life that are just hard, and during those times it's difficult to make sense of the hardness of it all. Each day seems to bring another dose of hardship that you aren't entirely sure how to navigate. If days turn into a season, your heart will likely long for life to "let up," and there may be a tendency to long for "The Good Ol' Days," rather than to believe that the best is yet to come. When these seasons come, take a step back and examine your circumstances with the Holy Spirit. If you look carefully, you will see there is One traveling on this path, called war, with you. His desire is that you trust Him enough to move from beside you to in front of you as your Leader, as the Lion of the Tribe of Judah! He wants to go out in front of you, as a fierce Lion, to fight your battles for you, roaring over every circumstance that desires to trip you up. Your role is to stay on the warpath behind your Lion Leader, follow in His footsteps, and resist the urge to run ahead of Him. Don't try to fight your battles for yourself. His pace is one of grace, so adjust your sails to the swish of His tail, and watch as He mops up all debris from the victories that His roar has scored!

2 Timothy 2:3   Psalm 23
Isaiah 50:4–7

Prayer: Holy Spirit, when arrows are flying to my right and to my left, and the north wind blows hard against my face, please help me to set my face like flint and stay in my place, the place marked with love and grace. Help me to pull from the reservoir of my past experiences with Your faithfulness and trust that even in this place, Your grace will save face. O God of Jacob, help me to lie down in green pastures and surrender to Your love and Your great faithfulness.

Day 82
Walk

Hut 2, 3, 4, what in the world are we fighting for? We are fighting for the upward call of God in Christ Jesus to be fully realized in each of our lives (Phil 3:14). If that call has been revealed to you and you have begun to pursue it, you have probably realized that seeing it actualized does not come without a fight. Fighting looks differently in different seasons. Knowing how to fight is imperative, and that is where a close relationship with the Holy Spirit is not only "handy," but crucial. Otherwise, we fight ineffectively as one who is "beating the air" (1 Cor 9:26). The Holy Spirit knows you and your enemy, and He desires to issue battle gear and instructions that are specific for each battle. Sometimes your instructions may involve something akin to "swinging a hammer," for over a hundred years while others look on and make fun of you (see Noah's story). Some seasons may be marked by making decrees, others by fasting, and others by spending extended periods of time in worship. Sometimes, though, your battle plan may be a little less clear, and in those days, you simply keep walking forward. During seasons of walking, remember that you are not alone. You must consciously walk hand-in-hand with the Holy Spirit, listening to His heart, trusting that even though you may not be doing what you would consider "warring," you are, indeed, on the warpath. Although simple enough to understand, "just walking" can trip people up; just ask the children of Israel. Walking seasons do not come without walking gear! The Holy Spirit issues very special boots for this season. They are combat boots that have been custom fitted to your feet with enough sole in them to last the entire season. These boots have a special name called Peace. Even though terrors may assail at night and arrows fly during the day, there is peace available to surpass your understanding and to keep your heart and mind through Christ Jesus. (Ps 91:5 and Phil 4:7).

2 John 1:6   Genesis 17:1

Prayer: Holy Spirit, please help me to walk with You in the cool of each day, just as Adam and Eve did before sin entered the world. Help me to give my concerns to You so that I, too, can walk without concern, in perfect peace, with my body and soul prospering under Your special care (3 John 1:2). Help me to be content to simply walk with You, trusting that walking is for the mature, who have perhaps already been through seasons of soaring and running (Isa 40:31). May this be a walk to remember with joy and fondness for both of us.

Day 83
Clean your Lens!

I just watched someone clean an acrylic glass shield. As the girl was cleaning, the lady behind the glass said, "Well, now I can see the beauty more clearly." This response made me think about how I am viewing life. Maybe I need to cleanse my lens because I'm not seeing things as they really are. Life's worries and troubles may be keeping me from seeing the true beauty of the day He has made. Perhaps I need the help of a trusted friend to cleanse my lens for me, because my vision has become too distorted to even recognize the possibility that I'm not seeing clearly. You should know that this revelation came to me in a waiting room. Sometimes when we have been waiting for a while, our eyes can become dim and our vision becomes weak or blurred. During times of especially long waiting, keep your lens cleaning solution at hand, and give those around you permission to help keep your lens clean.

Psalm 119:18   Matthew 7:5
Philippians 2:4   Revelation 3:18

Prayer: Holy Spirit, please help me to recognize when I need to "cleanse my lens," and help me to be open to receive help from others who may be able to detect distortion in my life better than I can right now. I give You permission to bring any area of my life into focus that has become blurred or distorted. Also, please show me if You want me to be a "window washer" for a friend in need of a little clarity or fresh perspective. Help me to wash in gentleness and in love, being careful not to scratch the surface of their lens.

Day 84
Super Ego

Lately, I've been seeing the phrase "super ego," as part of an advertisement. I've seen it before, but in the past couple of months it has really caught my eye and has morphed into the following prayer: Lord, help me to have a super ego! Now, before you skip the rest of this devotion and begin to think that the whole book must be heresy, hear me out. I think the word "ego" has gotten a bad rap. It can have a negative connotation, but its true meaning is simply one's self-awareness, self-esteem, or how a person feels about themself. How about you? How do you feel about yourself, really? While we are admonished to not think of ourselves more highly than we should, we should think highly of ourselves. How could we not? We have been bought with a price, we are the apple of God's eye, He has made special plans for us, we are the righteousness of God in Christ Jesus, and I could go on and on. As long as we don't grasp equality with God, and we understand that everything lovely about us is in Him and through Him, we are safe in our quest to ask the Holy Spirit to help us develop a super ego. Having a super (exceptional, splendid) ego frees us to walk in humility because we are so secure in who God has made us to be that there is no longer a need for others to feed our egos; we won't struggle with jealousy, and we will be free to walk with queenly ease in whatever circumstance we find ourselves in. Long live the Queen!

Psalm 139:13–14   2 Corinthians 5:21
1 Peter 2:9

Prayer: Holy Spirit, please feed my ego in the quiet place so that I don't require the praises of men to do so. Help me to know my worth in You so that I am enabled to truly love my neighbor as I love myself (Mark 12:30–31).

DAY 85
Antibodies

As it was for many, the year 2021 proved to be a challenging year for us. Both my husband and I fell seriously ill, and our bodies battled fiercely to recover from the impact of the virus that wreaked havoc worldwide. But thanks be to God, we both won the victory over that destructive disease! And beyond that, as we overcame, our bodies created antibodies, a powerful line of defense against future attack on our physical bodies. For our bodies to create these valuable antibodies, we had to go through the attack of disease. Without that fight, there could be no victory, no recovery, and no future defense.

Likewise, when we are going through an attack from the enemy, God doesn't always just remove us from the situation, but allows us to go through it so that in the end we have spiritual antibodies. Spiritual antibodies could look like discernment of the enemies' schemes, which allows us to recognize his attacks before they can bring us any destruction. Because of what we learned from a previous attack, we will have the ability, strength, and authority to defeat it. God didn't deliver Shadrach, Meshach, and Abednego out of the fire, but walked into the fire with them (Dan 3). As they were walking through the fire, their bonds were burned away, they walked out as free men, and through their testimony they defeated the enemy. Jesus never left them alone. You can be assured that if you keep God in the midst of your situation, keep your eyes on Him, and stay in His will, He will be with you in whatever you're going through. He will be with you in the midst of your battle, not just rooting for you from a distance.

After you go through a hard attack from the enemy, even if it's the kind that almost takes your life and shakes you to your core, you will survive and come out of it equipped with spiritual antibodies that will help protect you from future attacks. Lessons learned will make you more resistant to the weapons of the enemy. He may try to attack you with a different variant of a previous attack, but you will have the strength to withstand those variants. Situations that previously had the power to shake you badly won't even move you, let alone destroy you. Now you have authority and jurisdiction over that which the enemy tried to use to destroy you.

ECCLESIASTES 7:3   ECCLESIASTES 7:8
JOB 5:19

Prayer: Holy Spirit, thank you for spiritual antibodies that have been developed from previous battles fought and won with You. When I am in the midst of a harsh battle, please help me to remember, and draw from, lessons learned from previous attacks. Help me to teach others what I have learned with love, patience, and compassion.

Day 86

Scent

Today, like every morning, my love, my husband, was up ahead of me getting ready for the day. He started brewing coffee, took a shower, put on cologne, and was ready to leave. But before he slipped out of the door, he came and gave me a hug and a kiss. Then, he left the room and the house, and, yet, I still smelled his fragrance. Not only was it in the air, but it was also on my skin from when I hugged him. I smelled like him.

As I was enjoying his comforting scent, I heard a gentle whisper from the Spirit of the Lord saying, "If you spend time with Me and get close to Me, My scent will also remain with you, and not just with you, but people around you will smell My fragrance. Above that, the same aroma that is a comfort to you will keep your enemies far from you; they won't even come near you as long as they can smell My fragrance on you."

Only those who continuously draw near to Him, over and over again, carry His fragrance continuously. Just as I smelled less and less like my husband's cologne as the day wore on, when we spend less time in the presence of God, we begin to smell more like us and less like Him. We must return to His loving arms daily to spend time with Him if we expect His fragrance to rub off on us. As we abide with Him in close proximity, we will emit the fragrance of a life-giving perfume to those that are being saved and sanctified.

2 Corinthians 2:15–16   Ephesians 5:1–2

Prayer: Holy Spirit, please help me to be conscious of Your abiding presence with me and help me to abide with You throughout my day. Cause my abiding to be so constant that I am an imitator of You without even having to consciously try. May the sweetness of the fragrance that I emit cause many to be attracted to the One that I adore.

Day 87

The Day After

In my world, it's December 26th and Post Christmas Blues are threatening. Actually, they've been breathing down my neck for the past couple of weeks. By nature, I'm a "preparer," and I realized something important today. Much of what I love about Christmas is getting ready for it: the plans and preparations, from decorating to gift buying, and party planning. Once most of the preparations have been made, it sets in that Christmas Day will soon arrive and then, in the twinkling of an eye, it will be over. In the middle of this unlikely day to write a devotion, I felt the pull to do so. As I began to write, I was reminded that Jesus, too, is a preparer. He, Himself, said that He has gone to prepare a place for us. As I pondered this, I felt a prayer develop in my heart, and I knew it was a prayer He wanted me to share with you. Do I feel inspired, or even emotional, by the prayer that has been given? No, I do not. Do I believe the Holy Spirit has asked me to pray this prayer? Yes, I do. That being said, I have enough experience with this Helper of ours to know that if we ask Him, He will help us in the request and inspire passion for it, even though we may not feel it at the time.

John 14:1-4   1 Corinthians 15:50-55

Prayer: Holy Spirit, please help me to become passionate about preparing my heart for Heaven, the place that Jesus has gone to prepare for me. Help me to undertake the preparations with Your guidance and wisdom.

Day 88
Fly High

It's the wind that empowers the kite to soar to great heights and perform beautiful acrobatics in the sky. Without it, the kite lies lifeless on the ground. Don't fear the winds of change; they indicate the end of a season. They are necessary and provide the best fuel for flying high and expressing everything that has been learned in the previous season. They provide the perfect conditions for a recital, of sorts. During a particularly hard season, I heard the Holy Spirit speak this to my heart: "No matter how 'provoked' the winds become, remember that I am your Master Kite Flyer, and I not only guide you through the winds of change, but I also control every puff of wind that comes your way. Remind yourself that we are tethered together, and even gale force winds cannot snatch you from My careful hand. Kite flying is a dance. I release string to allow you to fly higher and I reel you in, closer to Me, when necessary. When it's 'recital time,' I give you more freedom of expression, trusting that you can handle being given more string to enhance your fearless dance through the sky. Remain secure in the knowledge that we are still tethered together and that I will never leave you nor forsake you (Deut 31:6). With the shifting season, I guide you through the blue skies with gentle twists and turns of My hand. Remain sensitive to My guidance, and remember that I guide you, but I control the wind. Do not fear that which was created to enable you to soar!"

Matthew 8:27   Amos 4:13   Psalm 32:8

Prayer: Holy Spirit, when it's my time to transition into a new season, and the winds are contrary, please help me not to nose dive. Help me to trust that You are not unaware, and that You are controlling the winds that seem out of control. Help me to rest in the knowledge that You care for me, even if I don't sense it with my physical senses for a time. And when the winds howl, help me to discern Your voice within their roar and respond to whatever I hear.

Day 89
Recital

After I wrote yesterday's devotion, thoughts of my last piano recital ran through my mind. I was in numerous recitals as a young girl, mostly dance and piano. The dance recitals were a joy; the piano recitals were not. It should have been evident to both my mother and my piano teacher, Mrs. Jackson, that I was no Mozart. Nevertheless, I took piano lessons for several years. The last year I took lessons, I wanted to learn to play "The Entertainer." I literally worked all year long to learn that one piece and finally had it recital ready. Toward the end of the year, Mrs. Jackson decided that she wanted me to play another piece at the recital, a classical piece. THERE WAS NO WAY I was going to learn it before the recital, and I didn't, not even close! And yet, right there on the Recital Program was my name with Beethoven's "Romanze" beside it. I am a little surprised that my younger self did this, but I told my teacher, at the last minute, that I was not going to play the classical piece. She must have come to her senses, because she didn't give me any grief over my declaration.

Rest assured that our Jesus knows EXACTLY what we are capable of in terms of our "recital." He will never ask us to soar to heights that we aren't ready for. I have often heard it said (in reference to God), that the Teacher is quiet during the test. While I understand the sentiment of the statement, this morning the Holy Spirit showed me that the reason He is quiet is not to punish me, but to sit and enjoy the exhibition of what I have learned under His tutelage and careful hand. If you find yourself at the end of a season, performing what seems like a solo for a recital, remember that your Teacher is right there with you, cheering you on, and enjoying your "performance," because He KNOWS you are ready. And remember, if you don't feel you are hearing Him speak during the recital, He is guiding you with His eye upon you. Just as we have faith in Him, He has faith in us.

Psalm 18:35   Genesis 28:15
Zephaniah 3:17   Psalm 32:8

Prayer: Holy Spirit, please help me to rise to the occasion and pray as I should so that I am prepared for my "recital." Please shod my feet with the preparation of the gospel of peace so that I maintain my peace as I play through each "piece" of this momentous season. Help me to "play" from a position of rest and help me to remember that You have trained my hands for war and my fingers for battle (Eph 6:15 and Ps 144:1).

DAY 90
Grace

This morning the words "fall from grace" ran through my mind. In the past, when I've heard that phrase, it was usually in reference to a preacher who had gotten involved in an adulterous relationship or some other sort of unsavory behavior. Today, I knew that wasn't what the Holy Spirit was referring to. Instead, it was an encouragement for us to not "fall from grace" in our daily walk with Him. As we close our 90-day journey together, I encourage you to be careful not to fall short of the grace of God by turning to lesser gods, or the arm of your flesh, for your rescue or help. Remember that our Jesus is a patient and kind teacher Who will not ask you to believe on His grace for something that He hasn't equipped you to believe for. I'd like to close this book with a scripture that I personalize and have spoken over myself many times when I felt stretched to relax and wait on the grace of God to appear. In brackets, you will find extra wording that I include with the verse when I am declaring it over myself.

> **"No temptation** [to unbelief or works of the flesh] **has overtaken me but such as is common to man; and God is faithful, Who will not allow me to be tempted** [to unbelief or works of the flesh] **beyond what I am able, but with the temptation** [to unbelief or works of the flesh] **will provide the way of escape** [the grace escape] **that I may be able to endure it."**
> 1 Corinthians 10:13 NASB

Prayer: Holy Spirit, please help me to remember that I am saved from all difficulties in life through faith in Your grace to come to my rescue. Help me to grow in believing on the grace of God, not only for safe passage to Heaven, but for every need that I have. Thank You for the beauty of the Gospel; the good news that I don't have to try to save myself from troubles or difficulties, so please help me to stop trying.

Help me to fall more in love with You each day and become more and more confident of Your love for me so that I am able to trust that Your grace will indeed appear and never disappoint.

> **In closing, do not discount the grace of God.**
> **He paid full price for a full salvation.**

90 Days of Devotions and Prayers

Lioness Rising Ladies' Ministry
LIVING WATERS WORLD OUTREACH CENTER
FERNANDINA BEACH, FL

Over eleven years ago, during a time in worship, the Holy Spirit asked one of our women to begin a weekly gathering of ladies called *Lioness Rising*. Each week the ladies spend time together in worship, followed by a message brought by one of the women in our congregation, or an occasional guest speaker. In addition to meeting weekly, we support each other during life's happiest and most challenging moments.

If you are ever in our area, we would love to have you join us at 6:30 pm on Thursdays in the sanctuary of Living Waters World Outreach Center in Fernandina Beach, Florida.

Made in the USA
Columbia, SC
05 January 2025